Essays on India's Political Economy

PRAKASH SARANGI

KNOWLEDGE WORLD

KW Publishers Pvt Ltd
New Delhi

ISBN 978-93-83649-28-0

Published in India by Kalpana Shukla

KNOWLEDGE WORLD
KW Publishers Pvt Ltd
4676/21, First Floor, Ansari Road, Daryaganj, New Delhi 110002
Phone: +91 11 23263498/43528107
Email: knowledgeworld@vsnl.net • www.kwpub.com

Printed and Bound in India

2011 FPBA BEST PUBLISHERS AWARD (ENGLISH)

Contents

Acknowledgements

These essays were written primarily for my students at the Southern Methodist University, Dallas, Texas, where I was a Visiting Professor during 2011. When I searched for possible readings on India's Political Economy for someone who was not too familiar with the Indian politics, I could find only a few. A comprehensive overview of the subject since India's independence, especially from the perspective of a political scientist, was simply not available to a student. This prompted me to write these essays in a simple, precise and lucid language. Therefore, this monograph is dedicated to the students and colleagues at the SMU's Department of Political Science and John G. Tower Centre for Political Studies. I am particularly grateful to Professors Harold W. Stanley, James F. Hollifield and Dennis S. Ippolito for making this trip possible. I am thankful to several other colleagues who made my stay in Dallas comfortable and to name a few, Seyom Brown, Hiroki Takeuchi, Stephen K. Wegren, Christine Carberry and Linda Robertson.

I am also grateful to the University of Hyderabad for granting me sabbatical to spend a year at the SMU. I am especially thankful to the then Vice-Chancellor, Prof. Seyed E. Hasnain, for sparing me from the position of Pro-Vice-Chancellor at a critical time to enable me to stick to my schedule. I have presented parts of this monograph at several institutions: as a public lecture at Dallas under the auspices of John G. Tower Centre for Political Studies; Prof. S.C. Dash Memorial Lecture, Utkal University; Fulbright Alumni Conference, Kathmandu; Conference on Inequality organised by NKC Centre for Development Studies; Prof. N.R. Deshpande Memorial Lecture, University of Pune; Central University of Gujarat, Gandhinagar; and the Centre of Multi-level Federalism, Institute of Social Studies, New Delhi. I am grateful to the participants at these lectures/conferences for their comments. I am thankful to my colleague, Prof. K.C. Suri, for reading parts of the manuscript and for giving very thoughtful comments. I have learnt a lot from all these discussions and suggestions. They have certainly improved the quality of this monograph. All the shortcomings are, of course, mine.

I am thankful to Gitu and Seema for their ungrudging support for this project.

Prakash Sarangi

1. Introduction: A Perspective on India's Political Economy

The story of India's political economy has been told several times. Some have emphasised on the dominant role of political institutions. Others have highlighted the catalytic role of the economic environment. Still others have focused on the inevitable impact of class conflict. While each of these explanations may have its own relevance; they do not adequately explain the transformations in India's political economy. This monograph is an attempt to present an alternative model that is dynamic and robust. We hope to show that India's economic reform of the 1990s is not a sharp break as is often made out. There is a remarkable continuity, if the process of economic transformation is viewed as a function of the decision makers' changing calculus of political pay-offs.

Figure 1: A Model of Political Economy

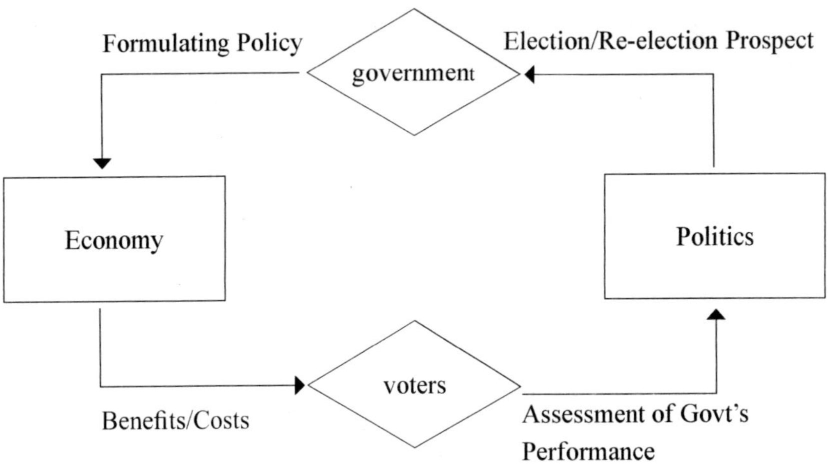

Political Context

Political actors and political institutions are important components of a polity. Political actors are those individuals whose opinion and ideas get translated into various alternatives for political action. This category includes, besides political leaders, important voices from the civil society, interest groups, business leaders and intellectuals. We assume that a political actor is a power-maximiser in his/her political activity.[1] The utility-maximiser in an economic market participates in a collective action which is a positive-sum game; there is mutual gain from 'trade'. On the contrary, the power-maximiser's collective action is a zero-sum game. It is a political game to control the decision-making process. By implication, a decision on economy is a political process and not simply an economic decision carried out by government officials in the name of 'public interest'. Every individual and group's propensity to a certain type of economic life defines broad contours of the economic policy. For instance, when a majority of population depends on agriculture, the state cannot ignore this sector. A significant concentration of vocal population in urban areas may lead to growth in certain sectors like consumer durables. If there is a sentiment to protect forests instead of establishing new industries, a strategy on industrialisation has to be defined accordingly. Every historical period has its contours of popular sentiment, which no policy maker can afford to ignore.

Social groups and their leaders, like individuals, try to mould economic policies and seek to protect and promote their interests. Their present payoffs and future expected payoffs become a significant basis of political calculus. Every political party, therefore, is sensitive to the issues of inflation, unemployment, welfare benefits, etc. Anthony Downs said very rightly that "parties formulate policies in order to win elections, rather than win elections in order to formulate policies."[2] For example, given the people's expectations in a post-colonial context, Nehru's strategy to use economic nationalism as a model of development seems to be consistent with the Downsian analysis.[3]

The role of institutions in determining socio-political outcomes is well recognised.[4] The institutional structures not only include the formal rules of the game (constitution, laws, etc.), but also socio-cultural contexts which give the rules specific meanings. The formal decision makers—like the ministers, bureaucrats or advisors—are endogenous to this structure, i.e., the decision-makers' behaviour is determined by the system as a whole. Their decisions reflect not only a broad social consensus on the issues involved, but also their perceived political implications.

The government (and party/parties forming the government) has a special role similar to that of a monopolist, though for a limited period. Its payoff, in the short run, lies in maximising the probability of its re-election. 'Appropriate' economic policy is an important determinant of this probability. By 'appropriate' economic policy, we do not mean rapid growth only. It need not enhance only the 'public interest'. Strategic spending just before an election can ensure a specific result. If a government is almost assured of re-election (as in the 1950s in India) it can afford to carry out its ideological programmes. However, no government—no matter how much support it has—can afford to ignore the expectations of the citizens, just as a monopolist needs its consumers to sustain itself. A government's strategy is, of course, subject to economic constraints, both domestic and international. Lack of adequate resources or overabundance of supply of inputs could spoil a government's strategy. Careful distribution of benefits—or lack of it—could bring bouquets or brickbats. Friends become enemies because of perceived loss, even if there may be no change in policies. The opposition parties wait in the wings to bank on the ruling party's lapses, if any. The competition among political parties is not simply to maximise votes; it is a fight over a policy space which yields enough support to sustain itself in politics and perhaps be a part of the government occasionally. Every political strategy, therefore, aims to formulate economic policies that are persuasive enough to mobilise a sizable number of supporters.

Economic Context

There is a symbiotic relationship between the economy and polity. "In all political systems of the world, much of politics is economics, and most of economics is politics."[5] A country's economic context is analogous to the capital in an industry or to the fuel in a car. It is a function of the economic resources available and the nature of growth because of economic policy. Neither the political actors nor the state structures may have any control over the available resources; but the fate of both is intertwined with this contextual factor. In fact, a country's achievements are often determined by a successful exploitation of existing economic conditions. Let us take the example of the agriculture sector. We cannot transform the geography of a region, which greatly influences the nature of products. Also landholding patterns do not change overnight. But political actors can generate social capital by organising the agriculturists for land reforms, subsidies, etc. They can help in the marketing and distribution of food grains. The civil society groups can create awareness about scientific modes of agriculture, thereby raising the farmers' income. The state may provide subsidies to agricultural inputs. It may keep imports out of the domestic market. It may not collect tax on agricultural income. All these types of state interventions could be reactions to the existing conditions of agriculture sector. Perhaps 'bullock-cart capitalists' as well as new political elites emerge because of the interaction of the politico-economic variables.

Economic policies use the resources for provision of public goods and for designing redistributive programmes. Taxes are raised and revenues are spent, resulting in reallocation of resources in the society. Political actors benefit by collecting their differential share of rent. Since each group in society evaluates these policies differently, they create new types of economic conflict and initiate social transformation.[6] These changes are often used by citizens as political lenses to assess an incumbent government and its leaders. When redistribution is too radical, it may arouse enough passions of citizens to organise, protest or overthrow a government. Economic policies may transform the nature of politics itself.

Thus there is a symbiotic relationship between polity and economy. Political economy tries to capture and synthesise this relationship.[7] Political forces influence economic choices and economic incentives shape political institutions and behaviour. This relationship is acutely visible in a democracy.[8] Economic policies are used as instruments to achieve political payoffs. On the other hand, political support—or lack of it—is used to manipulate economic policies. Economy becomes a handmaiden of political battles and politics becomes a victim of economic conflicts. We hope to analyse this relationship in the context of India since her independence.

Figure 2: India's Political Economy

Nature of Politics				
	Fragmented			Competitive Political Economy (1991-)
	Polarised		Populist Political Economy (1969-1990)	
	Consensual	Natonalistic Political Economy (1947-68)		
		Interventionist	Redistributive	Liberalised

Nature of Economy

Indian Political Economy can be divided into three phases[9]: (1) Nationalist Political Economy (1947-68); (2) Populist Political Economy (1969-1990); and (3) Competitive Political Economy (1991-) [Figure 2]. We shall argue that the first phase was marked by a consensual politics with very little challenge to the Congress party. This enabled the state to play an interventionist role in the sphere of economy—with decisions primarily by the elites—without much adverse political payoff. In the second phase politics was polarised and no single party could be assured of support all the time. The ruling party/ coalition indulged in redistributive economic policy in order to pamper a minimum winning coalition among the voters. The third phase is marked by uncertainty resulting from a fragmented politics, which did not allow any party to be assured of a winning coalition at any time. Seeking support from segments of population became highly competitive. Political groups found it difficult to calculate political payoffs on account of economic reforms. An inconvenient stand which did not yield expected popular support was quietly aborted. A competitive economy led to political uncertainties.

Notes

1. James M. Buchanan and Gordon Tullock, *The Calculus of Consent* (Ann Arbor: The University of Michigan Press, 1962), pp. 23-27.
2. Anthony Downs, *An Economic Theory of Democracy* (New York: Harper & Row, 1957), p. 28.
3. We need to note, however, that even if a democratic process takes into account individual and group preferences, the outcome may result in a common good which is not the specific aim of anyone.
4. See, for example, Douglass C. North, *Institutions, Institutional Change and Economic Performance* (New York: Cambridge University Press, 1990) and Peter A. Hall and Rosemary C.R. Taylor, "Political Science and the Three New Institutionalisms", *Political Studies,* XLIV, 1996, pp. 936-957.
5. Charles E. Lindblom, *Politics and Markets* (New York: Basic Books, 1977), p. 8.
6. Torsten Persson and Guido Tabellini, *Political Economics* (Cambridge: The MIT Press, 2000), pp. 6-9.
7. Various approaches to Political Economy can be found in James A. Caporaso and David P. Levine *Theories of Political Economy* (Cambridge: Cambridge University Press, 1992); and Adam Przeworski, *States and Markets: A Primer in Political Economy* (Cambridge: Cambridge University Press, 2003).
8. See, for example, Charles E. Lindblom, *Democracy and Market System* (Oslo: Norwegian University Press, 1988); Bruno S. Frey, *Democratic Economic Policy* (New York: St. Martin's Press, 1983); and Barry R. Weingast and Donald A. Wittman, *The Oxford Handbook of Political Economy* (Oxford: Oxford University Press, 2006).
9. The periodisation adopted here is not expected to be a water-tight division. There is always a phase of transition before a clear break in the old policy. For instance, some scholars believe that the first phase ended with Nehru's death and others believe that this policy continued till 1969 when the Congress party split. Similarly, there is an opinion that the liberalisation of economy commenced in 1985; while others feel that it was a failed attempt.

2. Nationalist Political Economy (1947-67)

Post-colonial India's primary goal was to achieve stability and national integration. The Congress party which spearheaded the struggle against the British rule had a mammoth task to lead the country in the path of economic development. Nehru as the first Prime Minister of independent India had the unenviable task to integrate India's polity as well as to secure its future prosperity. Yet he had a third important task, which was more important than these two: he had to win elections for himself and for the Congress party. Fortunately for him, there was no immediate threat of losing an election, at least not in the initial years. He could afford to devise a political strategy of generating a grand coalition of social forces, which he thought could help him to achieve the role of a nationalist.[1] He wanted his equation with the people to be based on a solid foundation: alleviation of poverty and raising the purchasing power in both rural and urban areas. The All India Congress Committee declared soon after independence the broad objectives of India's economic policy:

> "*Our aim should be to evolve a political system which will combine efficiency of administration with individual liberty and an economic structure which will yield maximum production without the concentration of private monopolies and the concentration of wealth and which will create the proper balance between urban and rural economies.*"[2]

Nehru had several advantages due to the unique historical context. His leadership over both the party and the government remained unchallenged, especially after the demise of Mahatma Gandhi and Sardar Patel. All shades of opinion were represented in the Congress party, which was able to play consensual politics, thereby reducing the significance of the opposition parties. The dominance of the Congress party allowed Nehru not to worry too much about re-election. He did not have to calculate the electoral pay-offs while formulating a policy. He could design India's economic strategy with a clean slate, without any ideological hangover, in spite of his own socialistic vision. These historic advantages enabled Nehru to pursue his 'nationalistic' goals in both polity and economy. He was guided by what he perceived to be in the interest of the country, while trying to satisfy all shades of opinion.

A 'grand coalition' does not last forever in politics. Consensus breaks down eventually. Each group/segment analyses the cost/benefit of a policy. Nehru realised this fact of politics a couple of years before his demise in 1964. His successors, Lal Bahadur Shastri and Indira Gandhi were acutely aware of the changing context. But they did not radically differ from Nehru's consensual politics or from the strategy of interventionist economy, till the context changed dramatically in 1969.

Economic Strategy

Post-independent India witnessed substantial doses of state intervention in the economic sphere. It could not ignore the logic of economic nationalism associated with the freedom struggle. Everyone dreaded the possibility of another East India Company entering into the Indian market, if complete free trade were allowed. On the other hand, the Indian capitalists, who supported the Congress in its fight against the British, wanted their pound of flesh. They wanted a protected market which would allow them to substitute imports by indigenous products. Nehru did not want to give them complete control over the process of industrialisation. He favoured the public sector to establish heavy industries with help from the international financial institutions. The state controlled key industries like steel, minerals, petroleum, etc. This 'mixed economy' was expected to be a synthesis of capitalist and communist forms of economic organisation. Nehru believed that it possessed enough flexibility and resilience to be better than both the approaches. He never imagined that his model of development would someday downsize either the public sector or the private sector. He expected both the sectors to coexist. The Indian state's entrepreneurial role was supposed to be critical to remove her economic backwardness.

Nehru's socialist leanings prompted him to give a greater role to public sector through the planning process. While his ideological leanings may seem to be relevant in pre-independence political debates within the Congress party, Nehru as a Prime Minister was quite pragmatic. He conveniently avoided any doctrinaire position while formulating economic policies. In a discussion on the Second Five Year Plan in 1956, Nehru said on the floor of Lok Sabha that while he was in favour of the growth of the public sector, he did not understand or appreciate the condemnation of the private sector. "The whole philosophy underlying this Plan is to take advantage of every possible way of growth and not to do something which suits some doctrinaire theory or imagine we have grown because we have satisfied some text-book maxim of a hundred years ago."[3]

Planning has been used as a tool to achieve specific economic objectives, both in the form of growth and distribution. Since the political executive has the final say in decision-making, planning has been essentially a political strategy. The outcome is invariably measured by the changes the government brings about in people's lives, not by the statistics of economic targets. Therefore, planning could be seen as the state's intervention on the citizens' income, occupation, group life, etc. It has a cascading effect on the citizens' attitude towards the state and government. It gives shape to their present and future aspirations. The goal of Indian planning has been to devise a developmental strategy and to give the country a structural leap from an underdeveloped agricultural economy to a developed industrial economy. The famous Mahalanobis model relied on capital accumulation as the engine of economic growth. It hoped to determine the rate of investment necessary to increase the national income to a level that assures to provide full employment. It also specified the various sectors within the economy in which investment ought to take place. The long term objective was to achieve a modern economy employing most advanced technology. Since it was not feasible in the immediate future without a local heavy industry base, Mahalanobis envisaged a transition phase which would rely on labour-intensive household industries for the sake of higher employment. Thus a careful balance was to be made between state-owned heavy industries sector and privately owned small industries sector. Commenting on the Mahalanobis model Nayar states that it "simply provided a theoretical scaffolding as it were for an economic architecture already determined on political grounds, without the benefit of or any reference to economic theory. In this perspective, a more appropriate explanation for the strategy is a '*theory of power*' .... instead of the power of theory."[4] [emphasis in the original]

A regime of economic planning was supposed to enhance living standards of people through increased production and expanded employment opportunities. The state was to play an active role in the development of industries.[5] A small but exclusive sector—for example arms and ammunition as well as atomic energy—was supposed to be under the monopoly of the state. A second set of industries—for example steel, coal, telecommunications, etc.—was reserved for the public sector but the private sector was allowed to participate, subject to government control and regulation. The rest of the industries were open to participation by the private sector but the state reserved the right to progressively participate and intervene. Besides the above, there was scope for private participation through cottage and small-scale industries. Nehru justified this compromise in his socialistic vision by the need for higher production at a time of crisis. But it was also aimed at giving business enough confidence by stimulating private enterprise.

India was cautiously inward-looking during its initial years of development strategy. Due to her experience of exploitative colonial rule she was wary of any dependence on the outside world. There was also an element of export-pessimism partly because of large requirements of internal market and partly because of being unsure of the marketability of Indian products abroad. The call for *Swadeshi* which was an important slogan during the freedom struggle became a rallying point to avoid imports and establish an indigenous manufacturing base. By adopting a policy of Import Substituting Industrialisation (ISI), India aimed to achieve economic independence. Nehru expected that the public sector would occupy 'commanding heights' of the economy by the state ownership and management of major industries. He did not want to give this leadership role to the Indian capitalists, not on the ground of lack of capital or expertise, but because he did not want economic power to be in the hands of a small group of persons.

Why did not Nehru adopt a policy of whole scale nationalisation of private sector industries? He must have been pretty well aware of the role of Indian capitalists in the freedom struggle. The Indian capitalists' plea for protection to Indian industries against foreign competition was actively discussed in the party. The Indian state was so preoccupied with the management of political transition that the public sector got very little physical or financial resources to carry out such a mammoth exercise of industrial development. Besides, there was a sizable voice within the Congress—ably represented by Patel till his demise in 1950—in favour of free enterprise. Nehru could not have alienated Patel who was in full control over the party organisation.

Private sector retained a substantial presence in India's model of mixed economy. Even while accepting a substantial role for the private sector, Nehru never expected this strategy to be a transition to socialism. Mixed economy has its own moral justification. Nehru thought that the private sector will provide stimulus to the public sector: "... it is advantageous for the public sector to have a competitive private sector to keep it up to the mark. ... [I]f the private sector is not there, if it is abolished completely, there is a risk of the public sector becoming slow, not having that urge and push behind it."[6] Nehru did not want a wholesale replacement of the private sector through nationalisation, though he thought that by controlling the strategic points of the economy the 'commanding heights' of the public sector would progressively supplant, eclipse and subordinate the private sector. The First Five Year Plan document declared, "The scope and need for development are so great that it is best for the public sector to develop those industries in which private enterprise is unable or unwilling to put up the resources required and run the risks involved, leaving the rest of the field free for private enterprise."[7] Given the background of economic nationalism during the freedom movement, Nehru was highly sensitive to the fact that there is a probability of a small group of people wielding economic power. Nehru's objective was to assert the role of political leaders in retaining power through the use of the institutions of state rather than giving it up in favour of the business elite.

Why did not Nehru use his socialistic credentials to formulate radical pro-poor policies? Nehru was singularly lucky to be extremely popular among the masses and enjoyed a fair degree of autonomy from the political compulsions of electoral politics. Interest-based political mobilisation was yet to come. However, he never wanted to alienate the traditional support base of the Congress party: the rural elite consisting of the rich peasantry and local business and urban middle classes.[8] These groups—which may be called intermediate elites—are generally risk-averse and therefore would not trust an Indian state which gives too much of power to the poor. They mediated between the Congress and the lower classes during the political mobilisation for the freedom struggle. They continued to wield that strategic role. Further, the rich peasantry, which was beneficiary in the first generation of land reforms, would not accept a compromise in its own economic power.

Unlike the policy on industrialisation, the interventionist state's policies on land reform and on rural economy were not quite smooth. The Planning Commission and the Union cabinet could formulate one centralised policy on mixed industrial economy since industry is primarily in the Union List of the Indian Constitution. Agriculture, on the other hand, is in the State List. Each state's socio-economic dynamics determine the nature of policy and its outcome. The redistributive goal was not clearly laid down in most states. The Congress Party was in power both in the Centre and the states during most part of this period and, if Nehru were really committed to a pro-poor policy, there could have been a uniform policy on land reform. "The national leadership's inability to enlist the support of [s]tate leaders for effective implementation of land reforms resulted in defective legislation that actually aggravated existing inequalities in the distribution of protected land rights enjoyed by land owners and those without land."[9]

Several Zamindari Abolition Acts were passed in the early 1950s by different state legislatures, but they failed to bring out the intended agricultural transformation. Many Zamindars continued to retain land under their direct occupation for personal cultivation, with no ceiling in most cases. They were often paid compensation for giving up surplus land. Even Jagirdars who had a right to collect revenue—and not own the land—were allowed to occupy a part of the land for personal cultivation. Many of these rich classes continued to be absentee landlords by entering into new tenancy or sharecropping agreements since the law did not require them to put in their manual labour as 'personal cultivation', nor it required them even to live in the same village. On the other hand, the tenants who directly occupied land were not given full ownership rights in most of the states. Zamindars did not mind evicting their tenants in order to show the land to be under personal cultivation. In many cases they leased out the land to subtenants as per the new law. "The fact was that the process of Zamindari abolition mainly benefited the intermediate peasant classes, those larger occupancy tenants—many of whom belonged to the middling Sudra peasant castes—who were elevated in economic standing relative to resident upper-caste ex-Zamindars left with reduced estates."[10] The position of actual cultivators did not improve. The weakest sections of the rural poor invariably suffered. The landless did not get enough advantage from the redistribution of surplus land because of faulty land ceiling laws. Even the Planning Commission admitted that excessive ceilings in state laws, combined with transfers and partitions of land had tended to defeat the aims of legislation. It reported in 1961 that ceiling legislation "was not likely to yield any appreciable surplus for redistribution."[11]

Indian planners envisaged the village community as the basic unit of social action. While the village panchayat was supposed to be the nodal point of implementation of rural development, it was expected to use a non-political organisational approach by involving the entire village through cooperatives and community development programmes. Initially the primary responsibility of cooperatives was to arrange credits and supplies for the farmers as well as market their products. Eventually they were supposed to encompass all aspects of rural life including cooperative farming. The idea of a community development programme was to stimulate popular pressure for social reform by addressing problems associated with low productivity, including basic education, credit and rural industries. People's participation was supposed to spur multiple social, economic and political goals of planning. Nehru hoped that the peasantry could be educated to realise their collective strength in transcending parochial identities to cooperate for economic reform. New leadership from poor peasantry would emerge in the long run to organise the majority for social transformation. These institutions, therefore, were not only expected to help in achieving the economic targets of planning; they could change the structure of political power in rural India.

The broad strategy of state intervention in economy continued for a few more years beyond Nehru's demise in 1964. Lal Bahadur Shastri's tenure was very brief and Indira Gandhi waited till she was well saddled in politics before she introduced radical economic changes in 1969. However, we should take note of one important policy during this period of transition, which had great implications for later transformations in the Indian economy: introduction of green revolution. During mid-sixties India faced severe shortage of food and aid from external sources was not easily forthcoming. Shastri took the courageous step to revolutionise the agricultural strategy. Instead of relying on institutional transformations in agriculture as has been hitherto practiced—through policies of land reforms, cooperatives, etc.—he adopted a technocratic approach to improve productivity by providing modern scientific inputs in the form of high-yielding seeds, fertilisers, etc. Farmers were given adequate incentives to market their products. Attractive support prices were provided. Food production improved dramatically.

Choice

The Nationalist Political Economy of India is a function of the interaction between consensual politics and interventionist economic policy. There are three characteristics of this phase of India's political economy. First, India emerged as an active entrepreneurial state. It guided and controlled all economic initiatives. It was not only a regulator, but also had a mandate to produce and distribute goods and services. Although a strategy of mixed economy was followed, the state was the final arbiter in deciding the type of commodities and their quantity that could be produced in the private sector. The state became a monopolist in certain items of industrialisation, which were reserved for the public sector. Nehru expected the private capital to be confined to the small scale industries and the cooperative societies. Those wielding political power constantly suspected the economic power of the capitalists. The issue was not Nehru's socialist ideology as is sometimes interpreted. It was a ruthless strategy to control by using a nationalistic state. Nehru had become pragmatic enough to think of the future of his party. The 'commanding heights' of the state were ordained to build 'modern temples' with an agenda to convert the citizens into the new faith of nationalism.

Second, Nationalistic Political Economy was guided by a vision of economic independence. Political freedom needed to be supplemented by economic freedom. Given the economic subjugation by a colonial power for centuries, it was a logical choice to avoid imports by following a policy of imports substituting industrialisation (ISI). It also conformed to the Gandhian philosophy of self-reliance. While the trade policy was reasonably liberal during this period, there was no visible strategy to encourage exports. Consumption within the country was given priority. One implication of such a strategy was that neither private capitalists nor the public sector undertakings faced much of a competition. Technological innovations in industries were stunted. This affected our defense preparedness as well. By the time of the Chinese aggression in 1962, the index of popular support for Nehru was on a declining trend. It was evident that the equation between the people and the leadership was based on the economic benefits/costs from an economic policy and not on an esoteric vision for the country. As the people participated in the democratic process after independence, their expectations from the state were also increasing, which no ideology could possibly suppress.

Third, the grand coalition that Nehru led as a part of consensual politics was in the long run a liability for his political legitimacy. The strategy of the Political Economy of Nationalism was to appease all, but it ended in satisfying none. Socialists expected that the state would take care of the poor. But the economic policy emphasised on production, not on distribution. Institutional models of agricultural development did not even address the issues of higher productivity. Cosmetic land reforms did not help real cultivators. On the other hand, the capitalists felt threated by the rise of the public sector. License-permit-raj took away from them their freedom to decide on production even within their own factories. Planning Commission became the new source of bureaucratic control. Although the recommendations of the Planning Commission were discussed at various democratic forums, including the Parliament, Nehru's charisma prevented anyone from questioning a proposal approved by him as the Chairman of the Planning Commission. Therefore, the grand coalition got reduced only to Nehru and his technical advisors.[12] The grassroots support for economic policies got eroded gradually.

Notes

1. Nehru realised much later that such a grand coalition is not quite viable.
2. All India Congress Committee, *Resolution on Economic Policy and Programme, 1924-1954*, p. 20.
3. Jawaharlal Nehru, *Speeches, Volume Three*, p.101.
4. Baldev Raj Nayar, *Globalization and Nationalism: The Changing Balance in India's Economic Policy, 1950-2000* (New Delhi: Sage, 2001), p. 53.
5. Industrial Policy Resolution, Govt. of India, April 6, 1948.
6. Nehru (1956), quoted in *ibid*, p. 204.
7. The First Five Year Plan, p. 422.
8. Stanley A. Kochanek, *The Congress Party of India* (Princeton: Princeton University Press, 1968), pp. 374-84.
9. Francine R. Frankel, *India's Political Economy 1947-2004* (New Delhi: OUP, 2005), p. 190.
10. Ibid, p. 191.
11. Quoted in Frankel, ibid, p. 193.
12. Jagdish Bhagwati writes, "India has suffered because her splendid economists were both able and willing to rationalise every one of the outrageous policies that the government was adopting, by ingeniously constructing models designed to yield the desired answers." Jagdish Bhagwati, "What Went Wrong?" in Rahul Mukherji (ed), *India's Economic Transition* (New Delhi: OUP, 2007), p.37.

3. Populist Political Economy (1969-90)

The second phase is marked by a transition from oneparty dominant system to gradual political polarisation. The competition was primarily between the Congress on one side and the rest of the parties on the other, except for brief periods when the former was supported by the Left parties, without however becoming a part of the government. Since the differences between the Congress and the non-Congress groups were not clearly defined by any ideological considerations, each group devised its own winning coalition. A party promised benefits to its own coalition of voters by manipulating the redistributive policy. Indira Gandhi initiated this game remarkably well.

Indira Gandhi must have realised two important political facts very early: Nehruvian model of consensual politics had already broken down and that a grand coalition within the Congress party organisation was a liability for her. Those leaders who were feeling suffocated within the large monolithic party decided to quit the party and to question the leadership at both the local and regional levels. The stark results were visible at the 1967 elections, when the Congress party lost its power in several states and got a considerably reduced number of seats in the Lok Sabha—284 seats compared to 361 in the previous election. The erosion of support for the Congress was ironically, not because of the emergence of a stronger opposition, but because of the defections from the Congress. Those who were opposing the party from within could now bravely say good-bye to the party and oppose from outside. There were others who remained within the party, but could never reconcile to Indira Gandhi's ascent to the Prime Minister's position. This is true of a group known as the 'syndicate' consisting of many old guards who wanted to stick to their conservative philosophy. Indira Gandhi must have asked herself whether she needed a grand coalition to be in power, since she could achieve her objective with a simple majority in the Lok Sabha. She engineered a split in the Congress party, using the syndicate's challenge during the 1969 Presidential election as an opportunity.

The popular endorsement to Indira Gandhi's slogan 'Garibi Hatao' symbolised her promise to remove all structural impediments to the redistribution of property. She sought support from her 'rainbow coalition' consisting of Dalits, Adivasis, minorities and the poor; both urban and rural. Her dependence on such a coalition was inevitable, given her strategic alliance with the Left to oust the 'syndicate'. Nayar writes, "Mrs. Gandhi's larger design was rooted in a strategic calculation that the political mood in the country demanded change in a leftist direction. The perception of the direction of change demanded by the public mood was decisive in bringing about political change."[1] Contrary to the popular impression, it was Mrs. Gandhi's political instinct to generate a winning coalition—not her love for the poor—that prompted her to devise a new strategy. "If the perception had been that the public mood demanded change in an opposite direction, perhaps the leadership would have accommodated it policy-wise. In a political system where holding of office was a function of an electoral mandate, Mrs. Gandhi could not do otherwise."[2]

Indira Gandhi's political strategy changed dramatically by 1974-5. First, she gradually distanced herself from the Left. She must have been under pressure to demonstrate that she was not a 'stooge of the Soviet Union'. The Left groups within the Congress became weaker due to internal oppositions from a new group called the Nehru Study Forum. Her newest political advisor—her son, Sanjay—was not favourably disposed towards the socialist ideology. Moreover, the country was in the midst of economic crisis and high inflations. Indira Gandhi was advised by economists to take harsh economic measures for stabilisation of the economy. Secondly, a pragmatic leader like Indira Gandhi must have been aware of dramatic changes taking place in social stratification. Green revolution created a new class of rich farmers.

The groups of small and medium businessmen expanded, thanks to the process of industrialisation. Expansion of education brought in new sets of professionals. "Some social classes were becoming more clearly differentiated and were entering the political arena; these new classes tended to weight the political scales more and more towards the Right."[3] Thirdly, the success of Indira Gandhi's direct appeal to the people for votes during 1971 elections reduced the political strangle-hold of the intermediary elites in political mobilisation. It empowered the rural poor to participate directly in the national electoral process transcending their religious, caste or factional divisions. They were ready for independent political action for institutional changes to enhance their economic status. This was the beginning of their political assertion which eventually matured into a creation of their own leadership against the hegemony of landowning elites. Indira Gandhi—and later Rajiv Gandhi—reinforced these direct political ties while underemphasising the state and regional leaders.

Ironically, enhancement of political consciousness among the people was also the reason for the Congress party's dramatic defeats during 1977 and 1989 elections. The Janata coalition in 1977 and the National Front coalition in 1989 tried to revive consensual politics by appealing to all the segments of the population who were against the Congress party. In both the coalitions there were attempts to blend Gandhian, Socialist and Liberal philosophies. These coalitions were, however, bound to fail under the weight of their own contradictions.

Economic Strategy: Redistributive

The broad theme of economic policy during this period was defined by varying notions of distribution of resources in order to benefit specified segments of society. This is a marked departure from the Nehruvian period's emphasis on 'national interest', despite the façade of socialism. This was doubly important for Indira Gandhi in the late sixties. She wanted to give herself a radical image in order to maintain her distance from the 'syndicate' and to keep her supporters in CPI in good humour. It was a strategy of survival. But the marginalised sections of the society might have been flattered that for the first time since independence someone was addressing their problems directly. 'Garibi Hatao', therefore, became such a powerful slogan.

Indira Gandhi was perceived as a messiah of the poor and her economic policies during 1969-74 reflected this concern. Ironically, the Nehruvian policy of state intervention did not change; if anything, intervention increased with a proclaimed intention of giving benefits to specific classes of the society. The objective was to achieve growth as well as social justice, so that the benefits of development could reach numerically larger but weaker sections of society. It was felt that the banking sector in India, being dominated by the private sector, was primarily serving the industries and commerce. Credit for agriculture and small business was squeezed. Indira Gandhi got fourteen major banks nationalised, thereby bringing 84% of the bank branches under control of the state. Very soon new rural branches were added. Rural credit expanded rapidly and savings were mobilised. General Insurance companies were also nationalised as a supplement to the earlier nationalisation of Life Insurance companies. This was followed by the nationalisation of the coal industry, of copper and of refractories as well as the taking over of the Indian Iron Ore and Steel Company and several cotton textile mills. As a part of the same strategy restrictions were imposed on the corporate private sector. Monopolies and Restrictive Trade Practices Act enabled the government to curb the growth of large business houses. Industrial Licensing Policy was modified to restrict entry into big industries. The list of industries reserved for the small scale sector was enlarged. The scope of public sector was expanded. Foreign Exchange and Regulation Act was passed to control foreign capital. There was also a failed attempt to nationalise wholesale wheat trade. Even though the government had justified the policy of control over trading in food grains on the ground of building a buffer stock for an effective public distribution system, the policy could not be grounded due to lack of cooperation from the trading community.

Indira Gandhi's general approach during 1969-74 was to use the public sector to give economic boost to the lives of the poor and lower middle class. She emphasised that economic growth should be considered as only one component of a multi-dimensional transformation of society. Essential commodities were provided to the weaker sections, rural employment programmes were introduced and house sites were allotted to the poor. The policy of land reform and land redistribution was intensified. The Constitution was amended in order to enable the government to take over the property of the rich and privileged, including those of the former princes, without a threat of judicial review. The approach paper to the Fifth Five Year Plan aimed at "redistribution in favour of the poor, in part by providing the self-employed with the wherewithal to achieve greater productivity from land and also through a programme of land distribution and other transfers."[4]

Indira Gandhi's economic strategy during 1969-74 had a serious contradiction: she was not sure about the means of raising resources. She wanted to dispense benefits to her 'rainbow coalition' while simultaneously creating constraints for those groups who would provide stimulus to economic growth. Radical policies combined with labour activism alienated investors. Unlike a developmental state which used public sector to invest in agriculture, infrastructure, public enterprises etc., now a redistributive state exchanged resources for political support. "Indira Gandhi held her populist coalition together by channelling public resources to numerous interest groups—a case of largesse that cut into public investment and hurt economic growth."[5] Subsidies in agriculture helped only the rich farmers. Savings declined and investments in industries were eroded resulting in a period of stagnation. Industrial unrest, high corporate taxes and decline in profitability led to deceleration in industrial production. There was no help from exports or from foreign investments. Given the sharp anti-Western political rhetoric, Indira Gandhi continued with the nationalistic import substitution regime. The consequences of the Bangladesh war, a major drought and an oil crisis had squeezed the country's economy. Rising inflation and loss in production led to new sets of regulatory instruments. This led to an "increase in the degree of overlap and complexity of laws, policies and regulations; massive procedural delays; increased politicisation of the regulatory process; shortages; and the rapid growth of the nonproductive sector. Manipulators, traders, and speculators, along with their political and bureaucratic allies, prospered on shortages while production stagnated."[6] This economic scenario resulted in public unrest, student strikes and popular dissatisfaction with the regime. Indira Gandhi realised the lacuna in her policies by 1974-75 and tried to change the strategy. She consciously distanced herself from the Left parties. In any case, she did not need their support after her massive mandate in 1971. The impact, however, was felt only after she returned to power in 1980.

The Janata Party, a coalition of various groups representing various shades of opinion from Left to the Right, came to power in 1977. It resembled a consensual group like the Congress party in the 1950s. But there was no consensus on economic policy. Each group wanted to dispense benefits to its supporters. There were several Gandhians who emphasised on decentralisation, rural development and small/cottage industries. The Prime Minister, Morarji Desai brought conservative philosophy to the table. Charan Singh's Bharatiya Lok Dal pursued aggressively the interests of rich peasants. Jan Sangh promoted the interests of the urban middle class and the traders. The Swatantra Party wanted industrialists to prosper and the Socialists defended the working class. Reconciling these heterogeneous interests, while formulating an economic policy, was a challenge. The coalition decided to have agriculture and small scale industries as its thrust areas, thereby alienating many of its constituents. There was open hostility towards heavy industries, both in public and private sectors. Despite the differences within the coalition, there was remarkable continuity in their political calculus. Each constituent pursued Indira Gandhi's style of redistributive strategy: using state's resources to dispense patronage to specific segments of society. Nayar writes that "the agriculturists dominated the Janata caucus, with the modern professions of the middle class constituting the second largest group, while business and industry had only a negligible representation."[7]

It was not surprising therefore for Indira Gandhi to target the top and the bottom groups in the social hierarchy when she faced the electorate in 1980 asking them to elect "the government that works". Governance became the new slogan. Indian economy was under stress with rising inflation and severe shortage of coal, cement and steel in the midst of deteriorating infrastructure. Indira Gandhi had no choice but to boost production. This needed technological upgradation, which in turn needed high investment and import of technology. The state was not in a position to invest. Therefore, it had to depend on investments from private sector and on exports. Competition had to be infused in order to ensure efficiency. This changed scenario transformed the country's economic strategy. Controls and restrictions on the private sector were gradually minimised, thus heralding the beginning of liberalisation and competition. The government also became tough on the efficiency of the public sector enterprises. Socialism was no longer regarded as an objective of state policy. Making the private sector the engine of growth did not imply that interests of the poor and agriculture sector were abandoned. Various programmes for employment in rural areas, housing for weaker sections, rehabilitation of bonded labour, advancement of scheduled castes and tribes were actively pursued. Rather a new dimension was added to Indira Gandhi's pragmatism: resource generation for maintaining the electoral support from a rainbow coalition. This broad strategy was further strengthened during Rajiv Gandhi's tenure as the Prime Minister.

Choice

Polarised politics and Redistributive economic policy contributed to a Populist political economy. There are three characteristics of this phase. First, there was a process of deinstitutionalisation of political economy. This was evident from the way participation and economic demands were channellised outside the traditional party system. There was a generational change in the voters as well as the leaders. Post-independence India's youth, which was ready to participate in politics, did not find sacrifice for the sake of nationalism as a very attractive goal. 'What is there for me?' became the new mantra. Rural voters, especially from the marginalised groups, who had numbers on their side found it difficult to accept rich peasants as the intermediaries in politics. Direct participation as well as emergence of a new breed of leaders dissociating themselves from the 'national' agenda of politics transformed the nature of negotiation and bargaining. Many regional and state issues became politically salient and therefore leaders espousing these issues could challenge the dominance of the Congress party. This had its effect on the Congress party: state level leaders became prominent and they picked up economic policies which were politically marketable. One author commented on Indira Gandhi: "Mrs. Gandhi was a political creature. She did not pursue economic goals for their own sake. She had use for them only if, in her calculation, they were capable of yielding political dividends."[8] This comment could be applicable to many successful leaders of that period irrespective of party affiliation. Success was defined by the populist promises one could make to provide benefits from the state. If equation was right, a new political party could emerge overnight, with whatever label that was convenient. By the same logic, if the price was right, a leader could 'defect' alone or enmasse to another party. Even the social groups at the grassroots level started negotiating with the top leadership on the price of their support. This may sound anarchic; but it was the beginning of the maturing of democracy: the 'people' were realising the importance of their vote and asking in exchange for some benefits in the form of public policy. Referring to 1967 election, Deepak Nayyar writes, "it is possible to discern a qualitative change in the interaction of economics and politics" and that "electoral outcomes could no longer be taken for granted."[9] Political organisations were still polarised around Congress vs. the Others without any ideological or class distinctions. It was primarily a competitive populism which spurred this gradual revolution in rising expectations.

Secondly, the state was the source of patronage in this period of competitive populism. Whereas the Nationalist political economy emphasised on the overall development of the country, now political parties promised direct transfers to specific segments of the population. Any group that could promise a stable electoral support was wooed with sops of various kinds. "[A] state that was increasingly unable to mediate between conflicting interests and competing demands resorted more and more to a politics of patronage. This patronage, which came to be extended in a bewildering variety of ways, was a means of sharing the spoils among the constituents of the ruling elite."[10] It is not necessary that only the poor were benefited in the forms of food subsidies or other welfare programmes. Rich farmers were given fertiliser or irrigation subsidies. Businessmen got tax breaks or export subsidies. Easy finance was made available to them through nationalised banks. Even the loans were waived, if needed. Thus a statist model of development was replaced by a statist model of patronage. A state which was an object of awe and admiration had become an object which could be owned as well as could become a subject of bargaining and negotiation.

Thirdly, socio-political conflicts became more pronounced during this phase. Redistributive policy is a zero-sum game, given a resource constraint. While in the earlier phase there was accommodation of dissent, in this phase dissent was openly displayed in the political arena. Dissent often defined the possibility of access to economic benefits from the state. Those who expected but did not get the benefits from the state opposed the party in power. Deprivation was given caste, linguistic, religious or ethnic colours. The dissenters were politically mobilised to organise a new party or a faction within a party. It started with the Congress party facing opposition from the regional parties, making it a Centre vs. State conflict. The regional parties faced opposition from the caste or ethnic groups. The cycle continued since public money was never enough to buy and maintain support. Social identity became the basis of political mobilisation. This had an economic implication as well. When dissent overflowed to the streets, it dampened the spirit of public investors, which in turn had its impact on industrial growth. When the economic capacity of the Indian state declined, it tried to manage dissent by borrowing, both internally and externally, thereby further deteriorating the state's capacity. This in turn generated new dissent and the cycle continued, often resulting in social movements and violence. The conflict of rich vs. poor got transformed to a conflict among different social groups. The government which was supposed to be a neutral arbiter in such conflicts was unfortunately an active party in the conflict itself. "[T]he centralisation of authority and power at the apex weakened the institutional base of the pyramid, so that the ability of the government to mediate between conflicting interests was much reduced."[11] Rather the governments used state power to dispense patronage to a segment of the population and to enhance the probability of reelection.

Notes

1. Baldev Raj Nayar, *India's Mixed Economy* (Bombay: Popular Prakashan, 1989), p. 266.
2. Ibid.
3. Mary C. Carras, *Indira Gandhi: In the Crucible of Leadership: A Political Biography* (Boston: Beacon Press, 1979), p. 211.
4. Quoted in Francine R. Frankel, *India's Political Economy, 1947-2004* (New Delhi: Oxford University Press, 2005), p. 501.
5. Atul Kohli, *Democracy and Development in India* (New Delhi: Oxford University Press, 2009), p. 124.
6. Robert L. Hardgrave, Jr. and Stanley A. Kochanek, *India: Government and Politics in a Developing Nation* (Boston: Thomson Wadsworth, 2008), p. 425.
7. Nayar, op.cit., p. 340.
8. K.N. Subramaniam, "A Balance Sheet", *Seminar*, 304, December 1984, p. 38.
9. Deepak Nayyar, "Economic Development and Political Democracy: Interaction of Economics and Politics in Independent India", *Economic and Political Weekly of India*, December 5, 1998, p. 3125.
10. Ibid, p. 3126.
11. Nayyar, op. cit., p. 3127.

4. Problems in India's Political Economy during 1947-1990

Economists assess the success of India's economic policies either by measuring the rates of growth or by the reduction in the level of poverty or both.[1] It is easy to measure these variables and one could arrive at quick conclusions. These measures also help us to make comparative assessment with other countries. However, there is a possibility that we may be misled by such neat generalisations. We may not be able to capture the 'success' of a policy, if success is defined by the fulfillment of expectations of people. There may not be a correlation between the economists' notion of success and the popular notion of success of an economic policy. There could be several imponderables. A high rate of growth may be associated with a high level of inequity in distribution, making most citizens effectively worse off than before. Many citizens, while being comfortable with a higher rate of growth, may not like various aspects of governance. The income of the poor may have gone up, but they may not like any charities from the state. It is possible that a specific segment of the poor was unfairly provided with benefits in income generation programmes. The expectations may change when the poor become a part of the middle class. The possibilities of distortion in interpretation are endless.

In a democracy the expectations of people are not confined only to economic benefits. In fact, economic policies are manifestations of a ruling party's strategy to maintain a good equation with the people. Several parts of this calculus are: Who gets the benefits and who pays for the costs? How much of the benefit or cost does one get, especially, vis-à-vis others? How does the benefit/cost look like compared to initial expectations? Are there some people who get the benefits even if they do not deserve? Is the gain/loss short term or long term? Even if there is gain for a citizen, is there a notional deprivation, since the alternative party could have given better benefits, if it were to be in power? Is there a notional loss for a citizen, since a person from a rival social group also got the benefits? Is there a perception of discontent because of poor governance? Many of these parameters cannot be easily measured. But it is a fact that citizens calculate using some of these considerations while assessing the performance of a political party in power. The latter, in turn, calculates the perceptions of people while designing an economic policy. No government is guided only by the rate of growth or by the percentage change in the level of poverty. The economists simply use economic theory to justify the political calculations of the ruling party.

Economic policies in a democracy should be assessed by a complex combination of several parameters. Some of the examples are given in the previous paragraph. The complex web of relationship between the citizens and the ruling party can be disentangled by looking at the expectations and perceptions of actual benefit/cost on either side. These can be summarised into three categories: (1) economic security: whether people are better-off now than before and its implication for future years; (2) equity: the nature of distribution of goodies and costs in a zero-sum context; and (3) regime's legitimacy: whether the ruling party has done a good job, according to the perception of the citizens. It is not easy to identify quantifiable indicators of these variables. We will use them to assess a few major trends of policies based on available information, awaiting further empirical analysis.

Economic Security

The Nationalist Political Economy was thrust on the people of India without asking them about their preferences. Nehru was guided by the ideas of nationalism and socialism. Neither of the two philosophies accepts individual as the starting point of a policy. In spite of the introduction of democratic institutions, consent of the citizens was taken for granted because of the Congress party's legacy during the freedom movement. At the same time Nehru was smart enough not to alienate vocal segments of the society. Two examples of such segments are: rich peasants who had the potential to be vote banks and the capitalists, who continued with their economic interests in spite of the emergence of a strong public sector. The tools of planning process were decided by the experts. At no stage inputs from individual citizens or social groups were sought.[2] There was no public debate on the suitability of planning as a model of development. Getting the plan documents approved by the people's representatives in the Parliament was a mere formality. Nehru as the Chairman of the Planning Commission approved a plan proposal, pushed it through the National Development Council, Cabinet and the Parliament. At every stage Nehru's charisma did the talking.[3] Either there was no dissent or if there were any minor dissents, they were brushed aside. Indian citizens were never told whether and how much they were going to benefit from this economic strategy; or more importantly, who would pay for its execution.

Thus, there was an element of uncertainty on the part of individuals to calculate the costs and benefits of the economic policy. Referring to the Second Five Year Plan, Nayar writes, "[T]here was an *incongruence* between the Second Plan and India's political system of democracy. … [T]he Plan was an extremely ambitious goal-determined rather than a resource-based plan, imposing 'forced savings' on the community."[4] (emphasis in the original). The planners relied on large scale deficit financing and a higher rate of tax mobilisation. "[T]his implied new burdens on the public, especially in the form of inflation, and by extension, considerable political risks for the political leadership."[5] There was no agreement among the economists on the relative weight to be given to either the industry or agriculture, especially on the relative impact on citizens. Heavy industries have a long gestation period and, therefore, would imply postponement of immediate payoffs; while a focus on agriculture could fulfill vital consumption needs of the masses.[6]

A policy of import substituting industrialisation and export pessimism was supposed to protect India's national interest, without any dependence on capitalist countries. Protected industries produced over-priced goods, which could not compete internationally. India had already become a part of the world market because of her dependence on oil and food. In the absence of an export strategy India faced a balance of payment crisis. The net result was that the industrial strategy provided protection to India's capitalist class, not to the average citizens. It is ironic that the Nationalist Political Economy which was built around economic independence had to accept an uncertain economic future during this period.

The Populist Political Economy started with a struggle between the poor and the rich. The game started with an advantage to the poor, or at least it was so perceived. The calculation was that when the economic interests of the rich are controlled, including taking away their property, if necessary, the poor is going to benefit. It became a convenient plea to increase state control over the economy. It was an economic rhetoric, but the motive was political. The 'Garibi Hatao' slogan brought in a massive windfall for Indira Gandhi during the 1971 elections. She could never fulfill her promise and changed her economic strategy in about three years' time. But she laid the foundation for a new political strategy which every other party imitated: giving special economic benefits to her own supporters—an action hitherto considered as a corrupt or unfair practice became a part of India's political economy.

While there has been a nexus between economics and politics in every democracy, it was openly articulated and displayed in India. How did this nexus change the Indian people's perception of their own economic security? First, the concept of 'national interest' was replaced by 'aggregation of segments of interests'. Since each political party promised benefits to specific segments, each segment could also 'demand' specific policies.[7] This allowed individuals to take grassroots initiatives in economic policies. Since the new generation of citizens were far removed from the lofty ideals of freedom struggle, 'necessity' dominated over 'reason' in economic expectations of the people. Short-term local needs dominated over long term requirements. Second, economic outcomes became relatively uncertain, defying the predictions given by the economists. Populist leaders tended to make too many promises, often beyond the state's capacity to fulfill. This was compounded by international factors like fluctuations in oil prices or by crises like war. Turnover in ruling parties—both in the Centre and states—became fairly common. A ruling party could rarely fulfill its promises, which sometimes was interpreted by election analysts as 'incumbency' factor in getting defeated. Third, almost all the political parties during this phase believed that economic security for the citizen is to be provided by the state—not by the market, nor by the civil society. Such a statist approach had a negative dimension. It was wrongly presumed that a state's extractive potential was unlimited. Intruding into the properties of specific segments or unfairly taxing a particular class gave a wrong message that the state had the potential to violate anyone's economic rights. This had an impact on people's savings and investments.

Equity

A citizen expects a fair distribution of benefits and costs of an economic policy. Commitment to socialism was an important component of the Nationalist Political Economy. Nehru strongly believed that the poor and the marginalised will not be unfairly treated by the Indian state. First is the issue of land reforms. These were carefully crafted legislations on Zamindari abolition, tenancy reform and land ceiling. A careful analysis of developments during this period reveals, however, that benefits eluded the poor and landless. The power of the rich landlords was too strong to allow the laws to be implemented in letter and spirit. There was no political will to challenge their supremacy.[8] The Congress party generated over the years "its rural political and electoral support through local notables, many of whom came from the ranks of the rich and middle peasant castes and upper-caste 'petty and medium *zamindars*' found it extremely difficult to insulate itself from the pressures and demands of these powerful interests."[9] In fact, the dominant landed class further consolidated its position by additional access to resources through cooperative societies and community development programmes. "Failure in implementing institutional change had not only impaired the entire economic strategy, but produced social effects opposite of those intended. By the early 1960s, disparities in income, status and power between the large land-owners and the majority of the subsistence cultivators and landless labourers perceptibly began to widen."[10]

Second, green revolution further aggravated the equity issues in the rural economy. This strategy "not only increased interstate and interregional economic and agricultural imbalances, but also exacerbated socio-economic disparities among the different groups and classes in the countryside by benefiting large landowners disproportionately and further economically marginalising the small and poor cultivators from the process of economic modernisation."[11] Only a few richer states could quickly adapt to the requirements of technological inputs associated with capitalist farming. There were also regional disparities between the wheat-growing states in the north and rice-growing states in the east and the south. Inequalities widened between the irrigated and rain-fed lands within each state. Further inequality among different classes of cultivators emerged depending on their ability to take advantage of the new techniques. Persons with large land holdings could get easy access to a wide variety of modern inputs to increase production. They were the major beneficiaries of liberal bank loans and other facilities under the community development programme. Thus small landowners and tenants were excluded from the modernisation process. A new class of agrarian capitalists—or, 'bullock capitalists'—emerged in the countryside.

Third, several types of poverty alleviation programmes were launched from time to time in order to provide economic access to the marginalised individuals. Besides the programmes involving direct transfers, there have been attempts to improve healthcare, education, level of nutrition, employment opportunities, etc. These programmes expanded rapidly during the Populist Political Economy. Was there equal access to these programmes? It is well documented that political parties often used these instruments to strengthen their support bases. The groups which were vocal and politically savvy reaped maximum benefits. A substantial part of the resources were spent in the service delivery system, be it the bureaucracy, local politicians, contractors or the middlemen. Rajiv Gandhi famously said that only about 15% of the resources reached the beneficiaries. The net effect of these programmes, therefore, was widening the gap between the poor and the rest in society. Further, there have been allegations of regional disparities, especially since the 1967 elections, when different political parties started to form governments in the Centre and the states. A party or coalition at the Centre tended to favour the states ruled by its own political group.[12] The developmental state was never politically neutral among categories of people or geographical areas. The rational calculation of a planning process was defeated by the game of redistributive politics.

Finally, importance was given to the public sector industries to counter the rise of the private capital. This policy also had equity as a goal: the profit from big industries, instead of going to private hands, would uplift the economic status of the common citizens. Nehru believed that the commanding heights of the public sector would eventually usher in a socialistic pattern of society. The impressive growth of the public sector in India has been characterised by one author as "hegemonic" and that "its reach extended to every sector of economy".[13] However, it could never produce a surplus that was big enough for further distribution. According to one estimate, "the average rate of financial return on employed capital was 2.5 per cent." In some sectors the return was negative.[14] Indian taxpayers' money was used to sustain the loss making units. Since the objective was for the state to invest in capital-intensive infrastructure related and heavy industries, this was an indirect subsidy provided to the capitalist class and rising entrepreneurs. On the contrary, the high cost of production of various commodities in the public sector—whether it be textiles or textbooks, fertilisers or cycle tyres—did pinch the purse of the poor. There was no conscious attempt to devise a strategy for public sector industries to innovate technologies to generate products for the poor, say for example, rural sanitation, alternative energy or cheaper clothing.

Legitimacy

In a democracy the citizens get connected with the state through publicly pronounced economic policies. A state extracts resources from the society by using its coercive apparatus and deploys these to enhance its support base. Acceptance of these policies by the people makes a state's action legitimate.[15] This state-society relationship is assessed periodically by voters. Besides economic security and equity, legitimacy of the state in the economic sphere gets into a voter's calculus. A state would have a high level of legitimacy if it listens to the voices of the people, rather than imposing its will on them.

Nehru presumed at the outset that a dominant role of the state in the sphere of economy would be acceptable to the people. Indians have been accustomed to private or family initiatives in business or agriculture. Their economic interaction with a government/ruler was in the form of payment of taxes in some form, which was not expected to yield any direct return. Though the independent India brought in a democratic government, most citizens were not sure about their own role in public policy, except perhaps to elect a party, which brought in freedom, to govern the country. Different economic models of development were alien to most of them. Alternative political voices like Mahatma Gandhi's village economy or Sardar Patel's free enterprise had already eclipsed by the time new policies were formulated. Nehru never thought it necessary to 'consult' common people on economic policy and went forward simply by the advice from the experts. Murmurs, if any, were buried under Nehru's charisma. Opposition groups were too insignificant to be able to educate people on the alternative economic strategies. Nehru was lucky in the initial years to be able to use the state power to 'command'[16] the politics of economics. By the end of 1950s, as the people realised the impact of the Nationalist Political Economy, political consensus began to disintegrate. Voices of dissatisfaction surfaced. Those who did not want to succumb to the homogenising process of nationalist planning raised banners of revolt, which was reflected in the 1967 election.

The legitimacy issue became prominent during the phase of Populist Political Economy. There were several politico-economic issues. First, economic issues were discussed and initiated at the grassroots level, thanks to the newly established Panchayati Raj institutions. Voters started to 'demand' specific types of economic policies and developmental programmes. Questions were raised about the areas of neglect. Implementation of programmes was subjected to scrutiny. Marginalised people were not the only ones who questioned the government; even the business leaders participated in national debates and dialogues. Second, elections at different levels—local to national—were used as arenas for bargaining and negotiation on economic issues. No one understood this strategy better than Indira Gandhi. She appealed directly to the people instead of going through the intermediaries, as happened during Nehru's time. The people also realised the importance of their vote, that number was their strength and that they did not have to always go through their local landlords. The opposition too capitalised on this new awakening by mobilising people, capitalising on their economic dissatisfactions. Third, regional deprivations in economic development gained prominence. Political polarisations began to crystallise. A dichotomy between the state-level leaders and the national leaders emerged. Gradually, by the early 1980s, competitive populism on local economic issues replaced the idea of 'national interest'. A party which could feel the pulse of the people by looking at their economic aspirations was rewarded at the polls. Fourth, an extension of the earlier point was that a party had to fulfill its promises when it came to power. Governance did matter for survival. The voters started to assess the governments on the basis of performance, not on any emotional tie of patriotism or nationalism. No political party could be assured of a long tenure in office. Finally, interest dominated over ideology. Political parties emphasised on the winnability of an economic agenda. Even Indira Gandhi distanced herself from socialism. Perhaps her use of socialistic symbols during 1969-71 was an electoral strategy. Given the political context, she had to depend on the Left and had to pamper a rainbow coalition. The massive win of Janata party in 1977 was not because of the ideological position of the constituent parties, but because of the people's rejection of Indira Gandhi's policies.

Thus, the transformation of Indian political economy led to disintegration of the old consensual politics and to the emergence of a new era of empowered voters. This was only a stepping stone to a new phase of economy controlled by voters as consumers, a clear departure from an economy controlled by the state.

Notes.

1. See, for instance, Jagdish Bhagwati, *India in Transition: Freeing the Economy* (Oxford: Clarendon Press, 1993).

2. I scanned through several volumes written on planning in India. None of them consider the role of individuals, groups or civil society in the planning process. See, for instance, a sympathetic observer and an insider of Indian planning, Sukhamoy Chakravarty's book *Development Planning: The Indian Experience* (Oxford: Clarendon Press, 1987).
3. The Second and Third Plans, the two most important Plans of independent India, are often referred to Nehru-Mahalanobis Plans, not as Indian people's Plans.
4. Baldev Raj Nayar, *Globalization and Nationalism: The Changing Balance in India's Economic Policy 1950-2000* (New Delhi: Sage, 2001), p. 87.
5. Ibid, p.88.
6. Please see the dissenting notes by B.R. Shenoy, C.N. Vakil and P.R. Brahmananda on the Second Plan.
7. The concept of 'demand' vs. 'command' politics has been persuasively argued in Lloyd I. Rudolph and Susanne H. Rudolph, *In Pursuit of Lakshmi: The Political Economy of the Indian State* (Chicago: University of Chicago Press, 1987).
8. A few interpretations of failures of the land reforms policy during Nehru's time can be found in Wolf Ladejinsky, *Agrarian Reform as Unfinished Business* (London: Oxford University Press, 1977); P.C. Joshi, *Land Reforms in India* (New Delhi: Institute of Economic Growth, 1975); Doreen Warriner, *Land Reform in Principle and Practice* (Oxford Clarendon Press, 1969).
9. Shalendra D. Sharma, *Development and Democracy in India* (Boulder: Lynne Rienner, 1999), p. 108.
10. Francine R. Frankel, *India's Political Economy: 1947-2004* (New Delhi: Oxford University Press, 2005), p.190.
11. Sharma, op.cit., p. 148.
12. For an analysis of differential levels of poverty reduction in different states, see Atul Kohli, *Democracy and Development in India* (Oxford: Oxford University Press, 2009), pp. 15-16. Regime type makes a difference to the poverty alleviation programmes. This argument is presented in Atul Kohli, *The State and Poverty in India* (Cambridge: Cambridge University Press, 1987).
13. Baldev Raj Nayar, *India's Mixed Economy* (Bombay: Popular Prakashan, 1989), Ch. IX.
14. Jagdish Bhagwati, *India in Transition: Freeing the Economy* (Oxford: Clarendon Press, 1993), p. 65.
15. James A. Caporaso and David P. Levine, *Theories of Political Economy* (Cambridge: Cambridge University Press, 1992), Ch. 8.
16. Rudolphs have famously called this period as one of 'command' politics, different from 'demand' politics.

5. Prelude to Economic Reform

Indira Gandhi's return to power in 1981 led to a rethinking on the nature of state intervention in economy. It was not a process of retreat of the state; rather the state was given a 'right' turn, moving away from the earlier Left-oriented policies. 'Pro-business state intervention'[1] commenced—a significant shift from dispensing benefits to the poor. This was not a move to accept pro-market reforms. It was simply adding a different set of beneficiaries on account of economic policies, with ultimate goal of electoral dividends. Indira Gandhi's strategy was perhaps based on a calculation that "a realignment with the big capital may not be too costly, in part because the poor were already loyal to her, but also because state support of business may lead to higher growth and thus to lower inflation, an outcome that India's largely poor electorate may appreciate."[2]

There were several reasons for Indira Gandhi's rethinking. First, she realised well before the emergency that pro-poor policies without adequate sources of funding had disastrous consequences. The poor were unhappy because their expectations were not fulfilled and the middle classes were angry because their interests were ignored. Second, Indira Gandhi's political strategy to give economic benefits to one section of population was already imitated by several other parties, especially by those at the regional level. Redistributive politics has its own risk in retaining a continuous support base. If any segment is promised better prospects by a different party, the support shifts. Indira Gandhi must have realised by 1981 that her rainbow coalition was in the process of getting disintegrated. Third, one of the lessons of Green revolution was that personal incentives tend to increase productivity. A larger kitty of food grains could help to alleviate hunger. This model could be replicated in industry and business. A larger base of resources was needed for social prosperity. Fourth, a new class of rich farmers, businessmen and traders emerged in Indian society, thanks partly to the Green revolution, partly to the opening up of banking sector and partly to the expansion of small scale industries. This upwardly mobile class had the potential to become future mediators in political mobilisation.

The primary goal of the new policy was to maximise productivity. Indira Gandhi—and later Rajiv Gandhi—agreed with the assessment of India's big business that an activist state needs to support private business, remove inefficiency in the public sector and rein labour activism. Several steps were taken to achieve this goal.[3] First, big businesses were allowed to expand in several areas by removing licensing restrictions. Private sector was encouraged to get into certain industries like power, which were hitherto reserved for the public sector. Second, in order to finance expansion, liberalised credit as well as various forms of tax relief was provided to the corporate sector. It was also encouraged to raise resources directly from the public. Incentives were provided to encourage savings and direct them to productive investment. Third, special legislations were passed to discourage strikes and other forms of labour unrest. Fourth, the public sector enterprises were asked to be competitive by better capacity utilisation. New investments in this sector were significantly curtailed. There were cuts in subsidies given to redistributive programmes like public distribution system. Finally, India expanded her international trade. Incentives were given for exports and there was a steady liberalisation of imports. Collaboration—both technical and financial—with foreign companies increased dramatically. Though the licensing system was not yet abandoned, "rules were flexibly accommodated to the increased demands for imports during the fast growth periods."[4]

These changes reflect a new outlook that the state cannot expect economic prosperity while imposing restrictions on the private sector. Socialism should not be negatively identified with the absence of private sector. Indira Gandhi went through a dilemma—whether to delink herself completely from socialism and accept the process of liberalisation. "With her shrewd political sense, she sought to avoid—unsuccessfully—attacks by the Left, through proclaiming that these gradual and pragmatic measures within the traditional socialist framework were necessary either because of a crisis situation or because India had achieved self-reliance through the policy regime fostered by Nehru and her."[5] Rajiv Gandhi, however, had no such inhibitions. He conveniently abandoned the word 'socialism' and proclaimed himself as an advocate of liberalisation. Backed by a massive majority in Parliament, he presented an ambitious vision. But he brought about only incremental changes to his mother's pro-business drift, with the state as the main source of economic patronage. He was not ready for a paradigm shift to overthrow the old system.

How did Rajiv Gandhi dare to be a radical liberaliser? Young, technology-savvy and committed to modernisation, Rajiv was a part of the post-independence generation that did not have an emotional attachment to nationalism associated with anti-colonial struggles. He was worried by the marginalisation of Indian economy at an international level. In Rajiv Gandhi's own words, "Self-reliance does not mean autarchy. It means the development of a strong, independent national economy dealing extensively with the world, but dealing with it on equal terms."[6] He could afford to think differently because his regime was not facing any immediate economic crisis. There was plenty of food in buffer stocks, a satisfactory foreign exchange reserve and a respectable rate of growth. He could afford to present a radical image by providing appropriate support to the private sector, which would become a channel of economic advancement. The public sector was relegated to a secondary role with the task of providing infrastructural support. Indian businesses got further concession in licensing, taxes, tariffs, etc.; but the market was not opened to international competition. Rajiv Gandhi's government could not fully disentangle itself from autarchy. He got identified with the rich and upper middle classes. His attempt to roll back subsidies backfired. This led to severe challenges from the poor and middle classes. Left-oriented groups both within and outside the Congress party questioned the pro-rich policies. Corruption charges against Rajiv Gandhi eroded the credibility of his government. Since the Congress party's traditional vote bank was getting eroded, Rajiv Gandhi moderated his policy in several areas in order to bring back many of the key groups to its fold.

There was continuity and change in Rajiv Gandhi's economic policy in spite of the rhetoric of radical transformation. He continued with the state showing favour to India's business class, a process started by Indira Gandhi. State support for the poor was not abandoned, but the socialistic thrust was relegated to the background. The state role in economic growth was recognised. However, the policy did not change far enough to accept the autonomous role of a competitive market. The strategy of growth prompted corporate sector to invest more, which eased infrastructural bottlenecks. However, a highly visible prosperity of the business class easily alienated the poor and the middle class. The latter was also negatively affected by the high level of inflation caused by large expenditures in the public sector. By the time Rajiv Gandhi realised the impending loss of his electoral support base, it was too late. The Congress party failed to win the 1989 election. The next two years witnessed the climax of competitive populism. The economic system could not sustain the liabilities of a bleeding state. No political group was willing to own up the responsibility of any alternative, since the future dividends were uncertain. A radical restructuring of the economy was inevitable.

The Contextual Factors of Reform

Very often question is raised about the timing of economic reform in India. What was the triggering factor in 1991? Why did Rajiv Gandhi's attempt for a limited reform a few years earlier not succeed? Rajiv Gandhi's failure could be explained by his ambivalence regarding the possibility of opening the economy to competition. He had a limited goal in favouring the big business within the paradigm of redistributive politics. There was a backlash when his government tried to scale down the subsidies. His attempt to depend on ethnic political mobilisation backfired because of the handling of the Sikh issue and the Sri Lankan Tamil problem. In a nutshell, in spite of Rajiv Gandhi's good intentions to bring about a gradual reform, he could not create a political coalition which was pro-reform, or at least not opposed to reform.

Several international events acted as catalysts to speed up India's economic reform. First, the breakdown of the former Soviet Union was a big blow to India's international trade. India was able to get the defence supplies in exchange for its exports without use of foreign exchange. This must have created a sense of urgency in the domain of national security. This momentous transformation in the international scenario also meant for India "a loss of a military and a political ally, creating pressures to shore up relations with the US. As most developing-country leaders understand, improved political relations with the US, in turn, often involve closer economic relations, especially the opening of an economy to American goods and capital."[7] Moreover, India had borrowed her model of development planning from the former Soviet Union. The efficacy of this model was questioned by policy makers after many East European countries adopted the market model.

Second, China's success as a socialist market economy was attracting worldwide attention. India's democratic development paradigm was often compared with the Socialist China. Chinese acceptance of the market model in 1978 and her perceived success in alleviation of poverty led India's policy makers to question her inward-looking nationalist economy.

Third, the investment scenario changed worldwide by early 1990s. Thanks to globalisation, foreign investors were willing to invest in India. Stock markets were opening up. Indian businesses were ready to taste the adventures in international market. Formation of the World Trade Organization (WTO) was round the corner and India was a likely signatory. "Given WTO's requirements, it must also have been clear that import quotas would have to go and that tariffs would have to come down within some time-bound period."[8]

The domestic political context was also getting tuned to the idea of accepting some experiments in economic reform. First, two elections in quick succession, in 1989 and 1991, both with hung Parliaments created a sense of insecurity among the political parties. While making necessary noises against reform, the opposition was not willing to take a risk in voting against the minority government of 1991. The political groups were too segmented to generate any political alternative. Second, although Rajiv Gandhi's half-hearted liberalisation was not sustainable, India's political class was gradually acknowledging several positive aspects of that period: the high rate of growth, stable production in agriculture and reduction in poverty. Earlier resentment against reform was mellowed down.[9] Thirdly, Indian business houses were gradually giving up their expectation of state protection and getting ready to face foreign competition.[10] The newly constituted business association, the Confederation of India Industry (CII) was becoming closer to political power compared to the two older ones, the Federation of Indian Chamber of Commerce (FICCI) and Associated Chamber of Commerce and Industry (ASSOCHAM). CII represented India's modern industries, which were interested in exports. India's political class, including bureaucrats, was ready to involve the private sector in the policy making process.

While there was overall economic growth during the 1980s, an internal crisis was slowly brewing in the economy.[11] Current account deficits increased and receipts from trade declined. Flow of capital from abroad declined, thanks to a lack of trust on account of political instability. Growth in exports was not enough to tackle fiscal imbalance. On the other hand, because of increase in the limits for license-free investment in industries, there was a huge demand on foreign exchange. The real exchange rate was allowed to depreciate in order to facilitate exports. There was a rapid accumulation of foreign debt. While rise in current domestic public expenditures might have provided the stimulus to demand, these were not sustainable since the bulk of the expansion was coming from defence, interest payments and subsidies. Continued fiscal deficit led to a buildup of substantial public debt. Maximum part of government revenues were used for interest payments. The oil price hike due to Gulf crisis worsened the balance of payment situation. India had to evacuate huge number of workers from the Gulf area. Remittances from that area dried up and the export market declined.

This economic crisis resulted in a fall in India's credit rating. Foreign banks refused to lend and non-resident Indians began to withdraw their deposits. The government sold twenty tonnes of its gold reserve to enhance its stock of foreign exchange. The final blow came when the foreign exchange reserve in 1990-91 was enough only for two weeks' imports and India was on the verge of default. "In June 1991, with confidence in the ability of the government to service its external debt completely lost, the crisis reached the doorstep of the country with the downgrading of its credit rating and loss of access to the world financial markets."[12] By the time the 1991 elections were held India's economy was on the verge of collapse. This crisis was used as an opportunity by Narasimha Rao who had formed a minority government after the elections. IMF came forward with a programme and World Bank offered a Structural Adjustment Loan. Several liberalisation measures were pushed through the legislative process. The rest, as we may say, was history.

Notes

1. Atul Kohli carefully distinguishes pro-market vs. pro-business state intervention. Atul Kohli, *Democracy and Development in India: From Socialism to Pro-Business* (Oxford: Oxford University Press, 2009), p.144.
2. Ibid, p. 153.
3. Ibid, pp. 155-163.
4. Arvind Panagariya, *India: The Emerging Giant* (New York: Oxford University Press, 2008), p. 91.
5. Baldev Raj Nayar, *Globalization and Nationalism: The Changing Balance in India's Economic Policy, 1950-2000* (New Delhi: Sage, 2001), p. 120.
6. Quoted in Ibid, p. 122.
7. Kohli, op. cit., p. 167.
8. Ibid, p. 167.
9. Suresh D. Tendulkar and T.A. Bhavani, *Understanding Reforms: Post-1991 India* (New Delhi: Oxford University Press, 2007), p. 86.
10. Stanley Kochanek, "Liberalization and Business Lobbying in India", *Journal of Commonwealth and Comparative Politics*, 34(3), 1996.
11. Panagariya, pp. 100-103.
12. Ibid, p. 103.

6. Reform of 1991: Emergence of a Competitive Political Economy

The balance of payment crisis in 1991 forced the Government of India to seek a bailout package from the IMF. Stabilisation measures like fiscal tightening and devaluation of the rupee reduced the current account deficit. It hurt India's pride, since she followed a policy of self-reliance. At the same time, it turned out to be India's 'Sputnik moment'[1], which spurred her to go for several structural adjustment policies beyond the requirements of economic stabilisation. Narasimha Rao's minority government with a non-political economist, Manmohan Singh, as the Finance Minister began addressing the underlying causes of India's economic woes. The goal was to break the structures of regulation down within the country and to remove trade barriers with the outside world. It was a process of shrinking the state in favour of the market.

The Rao government's policy of economic reform assumed that macroeconomic stabilisation by itself was not sustainable unless it was simultaneously accompanied by a restructuring of the economy. As Finance Minister Manmohan Singh stated, "Structural change is inevitable in any society where there is rapid technical change and we live in a world where science and technology have emerged as the major determinants of power and wealth of nations. …[I]f our economy is not equipped to absorb… this technical change… we will be marginalised."[2] It was a realisation that earlier economic policies had failed to achieve the national goals. Economic reforms were necessary to achieve these goals.

India followed a 'gradualist approach' to economic reform. It is an "evolutionary transition rather than rapid restructuring or 'shock therapy'."[3] Often economists prefer a shock therapy since it quickly cleans up the remnants of the old system. A gradualist approach, on the other hand, encourages the group interests to retard the reform process. India's preference for a gradualist course was because of the compulsions of a democratic system, which required both economic prosperity and its political acceptability. The need for a consensus was emphasised by Manmohan Singh: "In a large democratic set up such as ours, the dilemma of a reformer is compounded in as much as he has to balance economic logic with political and social acceptability and carry out the tasks laid out."[4] The gradualist strategy was especially relevant in the context of the minority government led by Rao. The political parties have been circumspect about electoral reprisals in case of radical policies. Elections were due in two dozen states by 1994-5. Therefore, reforms were sequentially introduced in each of the annual budgets, after high-powered committees deliberated and made their recommendations. Consensus was sought by holding public discussions with key groups like organised labour and middle classes. Any hard reform which was likely to adversely affect any powerful group was avoided. This soft approach was generally successful since it was relatively painless. Initial cuts in expenditures on social sectors during the stabilisation phase were followed by large increases in investment in these sectors. Thus, the broad contours of economic reform were defined by what were economically necessary and politically feasible.

Fiscal Reforms[5]

Fiscal discipline is essential for the success of economic reform. The fiscal deficit of the federal government had reached an unacceptable 8.4% of GDP in 1990-91. The government tried to reduce the fiscal deficit by a careful pruning of expenditures in different sectors, including abolition of export subsidies, restructuring of fertiliser subsidy, phasing out financial support to the loss-making public sector units, reducing development expenditure etc. Fiscal deficit got reduced by 2.7% in two years. There were later increases in fiscal deficit; but it continued to hover around 5-6% of GDP. In 2010-11 it remained at 4.7%. The government tried several other instruments of fiscal discipline: the net bank credit to the government was reduced, the budget deficit financed by the RBI declined, the net external borrowings shrunk and the ratio of direct-to-indirect tax increased. The overall burden of subsidy on the federal government declined, although the subsidy on food and fertilisers continued to rise. Debt-relief to farmers was phased out. There was a ceiling on government borrowing from the RBI. The latter was authorised to auction treasury bills at market rates whenever the borrowing was to exceed this ceiling.

Financial Sector Reform

The goal of financial sector reform was to enable the financial institutions to properly mobilise and allocate savings to support the restructuring of the economy. Instead of being a hostage to fiscal needs of the government, the RBI followed an independent monetary policy to regulate a stable exchange market, which was expected to enable a steady flow of foreign exchange. Regulation on interest rates on bank loans were gradually reduced and rationalised. New supervisory measures were designed to assess the financial soundness of the banks. Fresh capital was infused into the nationalised banks to meet the new capital adequacy norms. Debt recovery tribunals were set up to collect dues from loan defaulters. Competition was generated among the banks by allowing public sector banks to raise funds from the equity market and by allowing private and foreign banks to enter into the Indian banking sector.

Efforts were made to reform and open up capital markets for portfolio investment. Security and Exchange Board of India (SEBI) was given the statutory status to regulate capital markets and government controls were withdrawn. The National Stock Exchange (NSE) was established and it introduced nationwide electronic trading that matched the buyer and seller orders. Two depository companies were created for dematerialisation of shares so that electronic records of ownership and transfer of shares could be maintained. Foreign Institutional Investors (FIIs) were allowed relatively free access to Indian equity markets and limited access to debt markets. Indian companies have been allowed access to international capital markets through the mechanism of global depository receipts. Several private mutual funds emerged, thus breaking the earlier dominance of Unit Trust of India with government support. The insurance and pension sectors were also opened to private companies, with a limited foreign equity. An independent Insurance Regulatory and Development Authority (IRDA) was established.

Industrial Policy

'License-permit-raj' broadly defined the earlier industrial policy. A license was needed to establish or expand any industry employing more than fifty workers. The post-reform policy abolished licensing for all industries except five sectors justified on the grounds of health, safety or environment. They were: defence-related industries, atomic substances, narcotic and hazardous chemicals, alcoholic drinks and tobacco products. The public sector's monopoly was restricted to only three sectors: railways, atomic energy and defence aircraft and warships. Foreign equity investment in Indian companies was liberalised and foreign technology agreements were encouraged. A Competition commission was established to ensure fair competition among industries.

Trade

The objective of reform in the area of trade was to inculcate openness and encourage an outward-oriented economy, compared to the earlier policy of protection and import substitution. Import licensing was given up on all goods except a handful of items on grounds of environment, health and safety. Import tariff was confined to non-agricultural industrial goods and was considerably reduced from 355% in 1991 to 10% in 2007-08. On the other hand, tariff on agricultural products were increased as per the WTO norms. While earlier India had restricted or prohibited export of several items, post-reform prohibition was confined to only a few items on health, environment or on moral grounds and restrictions were confined to cattle, camels, fertilisers, cereals, peanut oil and pulses. The control over exchange rate was another barrier on free trade. The government devalued the rupee by 18% against the dollar and gradually rupee was made officially convertible on the current account. India had freed up many capital account transactions. Now firms could borrow freely abroad as long as the maturity of the loan was five years or more.

Investment

India liberalised foreign direct investment (FDI) in order to get greater access to the international market, enhance the volume of investment and improve the technology of production. Except for a few specific restrictions, there could be a hundred percent foreign investment. FDI has been prohibited in only four sectors: retail trading (except single brand retails), atomic energy, lottery and gambling. There have been limits to foreign equity shares in manufacturing items reserved for small scale industries, radio, TV, telecommunication, newspapers, refineries, airports, air transport, banking, insurance, power, defence production etc. The limit of investment varied from 20% to 74%. Potential foreign investors willing to invest at a higher limit could approach the Foreign Investment Promotion Board. These new investments created a competitive environment for Indian industries. Indian companies have also become more efficient and improved their quality by transforming their own technology. Several joint ventures between Indian and foreign companies have also materialised.

Public Sector Reform

The presence of a massive public sector for providing goods and services has been an integral part of India's strategy of mixed economy. It has been involved in the production of several basic goods like steel, cement, chemicals, electricity, oil etc.; services like telecommunication and tourism as well as commercial enterprises like manufacturing of TV, scooters, textiles etc. Reform in public sector enterprises (PSEs) has been slow and gradual due to ambivalence shown by different groups, including labour unions. The reforms started with a limited disinvestment of the government equity in public sector companies. The government retained 51% equity as well as management control. This was primarily aimed at reducing the financial pressure on the government, without adding to fiscal deficit. The government decided not to use the budgetary support to finance investments in public sector industries. Sick public sector units were supposed to be referred to the Board for Industrial and Financial Reconstruction (BIFR) to generate a consensus on a viable restructuring package or order the closure, if the units were not viable. Later in 1998 the government agreed to reduce its shareholding to 26% and gave up management control over several companies. The chronically loss-making companies were either sold or closed down after all the workers were given their legitimate dues.

Labour Reform

Reform in the labour market regulations has been most difficult for any government to handle. This is partly because the high degree of protection that the organised labour enjoyed over the years and partly because of its political sensitivity in a democracy. As per Indian law, any firm employing more than ten labourers (twenty, in case not using power) is regarded as organised sector and therefore subject to multiple regulations. A firm employing more than 100 labourers has to take permission from the government, if it wants to close down and such permission is rarely given. As a first step, the government created a National Renewal Fund which was supposed to finance compensation packages to the labour if a public sector unit found itself unviable and decided to close down. In general, the labour has been realising the importance of a competitive market. The labour unions have gradually become less vocal and there have been fewer labour strikes in the recent past. Labour agreements these days carry a clause on productivity. Most court judgments have not been favourable to the idea of the labour's right to agitate and disrupt work. The judiciary's pro-employer and pro-government pronouncements have brought about informal reforms in the labour market as well as in the public sector enterprises. Some of these may symbolise a pro-reform stance: 'no work no pay' if a strike is illegal; a 'bandh' interferes with the fundamental freedoms of other citizens; an employer has a right to abolish positions which are not required etc.

Agricultural Reform

Agriculture has been the weakest link in the process of economic reform. One possible reason could be that the state governments are responsible for most aspects of reform in agriculture: land and water management, supply of improved seed and fertiliser, delivery of credit etc. However, this sector has got indirect benefits from economic reforms. Opening up of trade has helped agricultural exports. There is a rise in the private investment in agriculture. Unfortunately, however, public investment in rural infrastructure has declined. This is primarily because the resources of the state governments have been diverted to populist policies like subsidised fertilisers, power or water. These subsidies help rich farmers; whereas when these resources are used to improve rural infrastructure, the overall production increases, thereby helping even the marginal farmers. Now the government procures foodgrains on the basis of the recommendation of a technical committee called the Commission on Agricultural Costs and Prices. Earlier restrictions on the movement of major food products, including wheat, rice, sugar and edible oil have been removed. An integrated national market would help the farmers and the consumers.

Many states have changed the law on the marketing of agricultural produce through the state-sponsored Agricultural Produce Marketing Committee (APMC). Earlier, the farmers were forced to sell through APMC agents. Now the farmers are under no compulsion to sell through APMC. Local authorities can establish multiple competing market yards. Retail firms are able to procure the produce directly from the farmers, thus scuttling the role of the middlemen. Large retail chains, like Reliance Fresh, are able to give good remunerative prices to the producers. Farmers can even contract in advance to supply to a specific firm. The buyer may provide inputs and technical knowhow. This has led to a major shift in the pattern of cultivation in horticulture, thus leading to expansion of food processing industries as well as exports. PepsiCo and McDonalds are pioneers in contract farming in India. Another experiment is by a corporate giant ITC in establishing e-chaupals—or, internet kiosks—in rural areas, which has revolutionised agricultural marketing. The central element is a website which reports the prices of products in different markets in real time. It also provides information on farming techniques and weather in local language. The farmers use the internet information to compare prices in different markets and get a lucrative deal.

A New Road Map for Economy

India commenced a new journey in 1991 in her quest for economic transformation. It was a radical turn in her economic philosophy and strategy. The trajectories of this reform evolved slowly—and perhaps are still evolving. The summary provided in the previous paragraphs is indicative of the foundation of a competitive political economy. In a nutshell, the Indian state has been retreating from its role in controlling the economy. She had steadfastly defended such a dominant role during the first two phases: first, as a defender of 'public interest' and second, as a champion of particular interests. In either case, the state had an upper hand in deciding the extent of competition in the economic market.

Having allowed open competition in the market place from 1991 onwards, the political elites could not be sure of the extent of patronage at their disposal to be dispensed to their supporters. Given this uncertainty, they might not have been sure of a stable set of supporters who could be relied on for dispensing special benefits. Citizens and groups, having got used to a culture of competition, realised that their real worth is much more than what was being offered by the party monoliths. Smaller parties realised their bargaining power in coalition politics. Uncertainties of the economic market engulfed the political market as well. This political dilemma was reflected in the very process of taking a decisive stand on the proposals on economic reforms. We will discuss the politics of reform in the next chapter.

Notes

1. A 'Sputnik moment' is a point where people realise that they are threatened or challenged and have to redouble their efforts to catch up. This term first came to used from the time when the Soviet Union launched her first satellite, the Sputnik 1, and beat the USA in space programmes. This spurred the USA's future space programmes.

2. Quoted in Baldev Raj Nayar, *Globalization and Nationalism: The Changing Balance in India's Economic Policy 1950-2000* (New Delhi: Sage, 2001), p. 145.
3. Montek S. Ahluwalia, "India's Economic Reforms" in Robert Cassen and Vijay Joshi (eds.), *India: The Future of Economic Reform* (Delhi: Oxford University Press, 1995), p. 13.
4. Manmohan Singh, "India's Economic Reforms: The Experience and Options" in R.K. Sinha (ed.), *India's Economic Reforms and Beyond* (New Delhi: Anamika Publishers, 1995), p. 17.
5. Basic data for this and the following sections have been gathered from one or more of the following sources: Suresh D. Tendulkar and T.A. Bhavani, *Understanding Reforms: Post-1991 India* (New Delhi: Oxford University Press, 2007); Montek S. Ahluwalia, "India's Economic Reforms" in Robert Cassen and Vijay Joshi (eds), *India: The Future of Economic Reform* (New Delhi: Oxford University Press, 1995); Montek S. Ahluwalia, "Economic Reforms in India since 1991: Has Gradualism Worked?" in Rahul Mukherji (ed.), *India's Economic Transition: The Politics of Reforms* (Oxford: Oxford University Press, 2007); Vijay Joshi and I.M.D. Little, *India's Economic Reforms 1991-2001* (Oxford: Clarendon Press, 1996); Arvind Panagariya, *India: the Emerging Giant* (New York: Oxford University Press, 2008).

7. The Politics of Reform

The Political Context

1989 and 1991 elections brought about a new phase in Indian politics. Fragmented politics replaced the earlier phase of polarised politics (political groups were either pro-Congress or anti-Congress). Active political mobilisation based on primordial identities like caste, religion and community contributed to this new political culture. This mood was successfully exploited by the leaders of various identity groups to negotiate, bargain and extract benefits. Some of the groups with a numerical advantage ended up as political parties. Pluralist politics took an extra turn with a newly defined political space. New groups maintained their independence from any large party monoliths, thus making it difficult to predict electoral outcomes. The political game remained shrouded in uncertainty.

Ironically, the Congress party, which initiated the idea of using segmental politics, became a victim of its own strategy. Indira Gandhi created her rainbow coalition of Dalits, Adivasis and minorities to fight against the conservatives in her own party. Gradually others became smart enough to use the same strategy to pull the rug under the Congress party. For example, in Uttar Pradesh, Dalit votes went to BSP; OBC and Muslim votes to SP and upper caste votes to the BJP. The Congress ended up being the main victim of identity politics. The survival of many parties during the 1990s onwards depended heavily on their political linkages with one or several segmented groups. Social or regional groups, which felt that they were underrepresented in the political process, established their own parties. The emergence of particularistic politics has been instrumental in empowering many groups which were hitherto marginalised. The latter could find their own space in the party system with their newfound bargaining power. Every excluded group imitated the strategy of the included groups, thus resulting in proliferation of parties. Unfortunately, however, there could be no limit to fragmentation. Each segment further encourages its sub-segments to search for their political spaces; each sub-segment further encourages its sub-subsegment to articulate its identity and so on. For example, conflicts among Dalit groups in Andhra Pradesh resulted in two separate organisations representing Malas and Madigas with their specific linkages with political parties. This has prompted other Dalit groups to search for their separate identity as well.

Fragmentation of political groups has three implications for democratic decision-making. First, it resulted in the regionalisation of politics. Disaggregation of groups had a geographical dimension as well. An important rallying point for political identities has been that of a region or locality. Groups based on caste or other ethnic identities functioned primarily at state level. Since these identities have become relevant means of political mobilisation, even the national parties view their regional units as the main focal points in inter-party competition. Each state could be viewed as a separate party system. Now most of the electorally salient issues are of local nature. This has enhanced the importance of the state-level leaders. However, many of these leaders have become oblivious or ignorant about issues which do not affect them directly. The policy of economic reform is one such example.

Second, fragmentation has increased the frequency of coalition governments. Since 1989 no single party had been able to form a government at the Centre. No political party, therefore, had been able to set its own policy agenda. Promises made to its electorate are often overridden by the compulsions of negotiation and bargaining with other coalition partners. No leader can claim to have complete control over policy formulation. At the same time, no party, however small or minor, is totally powerless in decision making. Since a number of coalition partners are regional or ethnic parties, they are generally flexible in their position on economic policy. They are not prisoners of a single ideology.

A government with multiplicity of views can afford to take unpleasant decisions, each party blaming the other in a collective game.

Finally, fragmentation increases the level of uncertainty in decision making. In a single-party government one could reasonably predict the decisions on policies, which might have been promised to the electorate. In fragmented politics the parties cannot be sure of keeping their promises. They may be unsure of a policy position that would yield them maximum political support. Since no political party is likely to have a firm position on economic policy, negotiations with other parties for coalition formation becomes unpredictable. Even after the formulation of a policy, a party may not own it up since it may not be sure about its electoral fallout. Thus neither voters nor the political parties are sure about their possible payoffs from a policy. This type of fuzzy situation may indeed yield more dividends for a party, if it does not take a firm stand on economic policy. Not taking a stand in the electoral platform could itself be a political position. This uncertainty fortunately allows a government to take risks of venturing into untrodden paths without alienating too many people.

Changing Pattern of Democracy

Fragmentation of political groups had a profound impact on the working of Indian democracy. There was a participatory upsurge among different sections of society. Two developments contributed immensely to the upsurge. First was the decision to accept the Mandal Commission report and to extend the benefits of reservation to the OBCs. There were emotional reactions to both in favour and against this decision. Every political group experienced a political realignment on account of this issue. It also sent out a message to every caste group that, if properly organised, it could also secure specific benefits for its group, either through the electoral process or outside it. Second, the BJP tried to arouse Hindu sentiments by fomenting the issue of Babri Masjid and Ram Janmabhumi. BJP leader L.K. Advani went around the country in a *Rath-yatra* seeking volunteers to build a Ram temple in Ayodhya, which eventually resulted in the demolition of the Masjid in 1992. There were obvious reactions from the Muslim community, often resulting in riots. Both the developments reassured the political leaders that primordial identities, like caste and religion, could be successfully used in political mobilisation.

Ashutosh Varshney describes the above political activities as examples of 'mass politics'. "Because they invoke ascriptive, not voluntary, considerations, the effect of ethnic cleavages and ethnically based policies are obvious to most people and, more often than not, ethnic groups are also organised, or tend to organise quickly."[1] A policy on economic reforms does not arouse similar passions. It is confined to debates and discussions among the elites: bureaucrats, academics, journalists, businessmen and elected representatives. It is primarily the middle class who is affected and they hardly ever step out into the streets. The masses, on the other hand, are more worried about the fallout of their ethnic identity than the implications of economic reform. Varshney argues that the preoccupation of masses with street politics facilitated the passage of economic reforms. "The political logic induced by explosions of communal passions gave the reformers room to push reforms."[2] This enabled the Narasimha Rao government in 1991 to push through the reform proposals in Parliament, even if the Congress party did not have majority support. The BJP was less worried about economic reforms than the possible electoral dividends from the Ram temple issue, which were believed to override caste-based political mobilisations. The Left-oriented groups imagined the rise of BJP as a greater threat than the rise of a new capitalist class after economic reform. Congress managed the passage of legislations on reform without much opposition in the Indian Parliament. The politics on the streets, instead of questioning such a radical change, were of course preoccupied with identity issues.

Fragmentation of politics got accelerated with the emergence of the BJP as an important political player. BJP's philosophy of Hindutva or Hindu nationalism was a direct threat to secular politics practiced by the Congress and several other Left-of-the-Centre parties. The BJP tried to rely on the Hindu 'majority', whereas other parties tried to woo secular class categories like the poor or the peasants. "If the poor were majority by the criterion of wealth, Hindus were the religious majority. Appeals to the majority religious community against minority communities, then, can be an alternative strategy for seeking electoral majorities by downplaying class issues at the expense of communal ones."[3] BJP's collaborators VHP and RSS ensured that Hindutva continued as an active means of reaching out to the masses. This identity politics indirectly got entangled in the BJP's position on economic reform. Most vocal supporters of the party happened to be businessmen, traders and merchants. BJP represented these voices.

Politics by Stealth?

Fragmentation of politics contributed to uncertainties, which ironically ensured the smooth passage of proposals of economic reforms in the Indian Parliament. No one was sure about the possible winners and losers. It was difficult to calculate the future impact on the citizens. No political party dared to take a specific position on supporting or opposing the new policies since the reactions of the electorate was unclear. Hence, proposals, though radical in their possible implications, were quietly brought in with a camouflage of continuity. Rob Jenkins describes this as politics by stealth. "The understated nature of what has been taking place in India helps to conceal both the sheer magnitude of these reforms, as well as the chief reason why policy changes with such far-reaching implications could escape the political minefield that democracy lays in their path."[4] Jenkins suggests that there were few impediments to the introduction of reforms because of the stealthy means of their introduction.

The goal of any political leader is to win the game of politics. In a democracy it would ordinarily mean winning elections. But sometimes losing an election or winning a few seats may equally secure political payoffs. A political group may in fact gain by not taking a firm stand on an issue. A skilled politician would prepare a strategy which both reveals a party's achievements as well as hides its failures. This skill, according to Rob Jenkins, was very useful while taking a position on economic reform: "a talent for obfuscation, the use of intentional ambiguity, and the exploitation of other politically expedient means in the pursuit of constantly shifting policy objectives."[5] According to Jenkins, there are two ways these political skills were used to see the reforms through. The first skill was giving the appearance of continuity in policy while quietly bringing about substantive changes. This gives a reassurance to those who have been beneficiaries of the status quo and to those who may avoid the risks of uncertain future. This also allows the government sufficient autonomy from the diverse elements in society in order to fulfill its vision of change. Confusion is created by rhetorical skills, e.g., Narsimha Rao's attempts to suggest liberalisation's continuity with the past by equating it with the Gandhian idea of self-reliance or finding compatibilities between nationalism and entrepreneurship. Similarly, Manmohan Singh emphasised on freeing the market as the culmination of Nehru's vision of development. The second political skill which helped the smooth passage of economic reform was disguising continuity as change: "the tactic is to accentuate fairly insignificant areas of governmental resistance to the neo-liberal agenda, even as market forces are heading inexorably in the same direction."[6] The United Front government supported by the Left as well as the NDA government led by the BJP made symbolic noises of withdrawing certain reforms introduced by the Congress government, but never took decisions to abandon these policies altogether.

Ideology and Reform

Any radical change in economic policy is normally associated with strong ideological support and opposition. In case of India, however, this was not the case in 1991. The Congress party never defended the reforms as the new catalysts of change. The objections of the Left parties had already become soft after the breakdown of the Soviet Union and the acceptance of market logic by the Chinese. In fact, India never needed an ideological justification for economic reform. The economic policies introduced in 1991 onwards were not as radical as the Chinese experienced in their transition from the socialist to the market economy. Referring to Deng Xiao Ping's statement, 'to get rich is glorious' to justify market-oriented reform, Sachs et al write, "A market economy is emerging in China from the ruins of a discredited ideology. Because of the abject failures of the latter, getting rich could be officially and publicly termed glorious."[7] On the other hand, private business was all along a part of India's economic life. Profit motive in trade and commerce was never alien to the Indian people.

What is surprising, however, that while almost all political parties directly or indirectly supported and/or implemented different aspects of economic reform, no one ever claimed the onus of responsibility for introducing these radical changes. The Congress party had already abandoned the word 'socialism' from its vocabulary. It had experimented with a liberalised economic policy during Rajiv Gandhi's time but it never dared to openly defend economic reforms during electoral campaigns. So was the case with the BJP with merchants and traders as its important supporters. It had been in favour of reducing state control over the economy. Though it advocated free trade (at least within the country), it never brought the issue to the electoral arena. The political class never wanted this issue to be electorally salient. In 1996 only 19% (14% in rural areas)[8] had even heard of economic reforms, let alone forming an opinion on them. One possible explanation could be that no one wanted to take the risk by convincing the electorate on the possible positive impact on the society. There was already a perception that only the rich and the middle class was likely to benefit, at least during the first few years. No one was sure whether these policies could get more jobs or alleviate poverty. Using this as a strategy for electoral mobilisation was too much of a gamble. Rather, not taking a firm stand on reforms—either for or against—could yield better political dividends.

Changing Nature of State Power

Part of the reason for political ambivalence on the economic reform was that the state's power structure was changing dramatically. Deepak Nayyar captures the new context very well: "The rich dominate the economy now more than earlier, but the poor have a strong voice in the polity now more than earlier."[9] There was a lot of political fluidity in the 1990s as a result of churnings among the social classes. Pranab Bardhan's description of the three proprietory classes—industrialist-capitalist class, rich farmers and the 'professionals', including the bureaucracy and white-collar workers—needs some rethinking.[10] Political decision-making has shifted to the middle and lower classes. The upper classes moved to the private sector or have gone abroad. Now they have no objections to a retreat of the state even from the social sector. Bureaucracy has lost its neutrality and openly aligns with specific caste and class groups.

But the economic reforms did not lead to the state losing its dominance. The fact that the power structure could quietly steer the radical changes in the economy testifies to its autonomy and resilience. It is further corroborated by its unwillingness to move forward in certain sectors like labour laws or opening up of education or legal practice to the foreign competitors. Contrary to many speculations, social sector spending did not get reduced, except for the first couple years of fiscal stabilisation. Rather the state went overboard to proclaim its keenness to take up new welfare measures for the masses. The old system of state patronage and favours continued. The state regulation on industry and trade got decentralised. It might have declined a bit at the level of the Central government, but provincial states' regulation continued to grow, since they provided land and other infrastructure as well as looked after law and order. By coincidence, it happened at a time when regional leaders were becoming more powerful, even at the level of the Central government. The power structure, therefore, needs to be redefined separately for each state. Pranab Bardhan's neat categorisation of proprietory classes for the entire country has to be reassessed for each state separately.

Notes

1. Ashutosh Varshney, "Mass Politics or Elite Politics? India's Economic Reforms in Comparative Perspective" in Jeffrey D. Sachs, et al (eds.), *India in the Era of Economic Reforms* (New Delhi: Oxford University Press, 1999), p.223.
2. Ibid, p. 225.
3. Atul Kohli, *Democracy and Development in India* (New Delhi: Oxford University Press, 2009), pp. 194-5.
4. Rob Jenkins, *Democratic Politics and Economic Reform in India* (Cambridge: Cambridge University Press, 1999), p. 13.

5. Ibid, p. 174.
6. Ibid, p. 196.
7. Jeffrey D. Sachs, Ashutosh Varshney and Nirupam Bajpai, "Introduction" in their edited, *India in the Era of Economic Reform* (New Delhi: Oxford University Press, 1999), p. 20.
8. *India Today*, August 31, 1996.
9. Deepak Nayyar, "Economic Development and Political Democracy", *Economic and Political Weekly*, 33 (49), 1998, p. 3129.
10. Although Bardhan himself does think that much has changed after the reforms. See his epilogue to the 1998 revised edition of his 1984 book. Bardhan, Pranab, *Political Economy of Development in India*, 2nd edition, (New Delhi: Oxford University Press, 1998).

8. Poverty and Inequality after Economic Reform

The goal of any change in economic policy is to make the people of the country better-off compared to the earlier policy. In case of India the litmus test lies in the policy's impact on poverty, since she has an alarmingly large number of poor people. The experience of the poor is doubly important in a democracy. Their opinion translated through the ballot box determines the long term survival of the reforms.

Panagariya[1] presents several theoretical reasons for an association between economic reform and poverty alleviation. First, openness in trade gives a comparative advantage to labour-intensive goods. India being a labour surplus country could benefit. Second, a policy of protection discriminates against agriculture. A liberalisation policy would facilitate the export of agricultural commodities, which would help the poor working in this sector. Third, a high rate of economic growth would create demands for new jobs, which would increase the income of the marginalised. Fourth, a fast growing economy would be able to raise enough resources for poverty alleviation programmes. Finally, when a family's income increases, it would be in a better position to avail services like education or health. For example, even if free education is provided, a poor family may force the child to work rather than sending him/her to school.

There is considerable disagreement among the economists regarding the meaning of poverty, the definition of poverty line and, therefore, number of people below poverty line in India. The simplest assessment is based on income: the Planning Commission regards an income below Rs. 32 per person per day as below poverty line; the same figure for

World Bank is USD1.25. In either estimates, there seems to be a decline in the headcount of those below poverty line after the commencement of economic reforms. Planning Commission data indicate that the percentage of population below poverty line declined from 45.3% (1993-94) to 29.8% (2009-10). The World Bank estimates this decline to be from 54% (1990) to 32.7% (2010).

A Few Poverty Estimates

% Below Poverty Line, World Bank ($1.25 a day)	54% (1990)	32.7% (2010)
% Below Poverty Line, Planning Com (Rs. 32 a day)	45.3% (1993-94)	29.8% (2009-10)
UN Human Development Index	0.308 (1991)	0.554 (2012)
GDP per person employed ($ 1990 PPP), WB	3531 (1990)	8939 (2011)
Infant Mortality Rate (per 1000 child births), WB	81 (1990)	47 (2011)
% of population undernourished (HDR)	24% (1990)	18% (2012)
Unemployment Rate	7.3% (1991)	

'Income-poverty' may not tell us the story of the quality of life led by people. Nor can it assess the deprivations suffered by the people. For instance, a high income cannot always ensure sanitation, safe drinking water or prevention of communicable diseases. Data available in the UN Human Development Index and Deprivation index partly fills the gap. India's position in the Human Development Index has improved from 0.308 (1991) to 0.554 (2012). The percentage of the undernourished population has declined from 24% (1990) to 18% (2012). The World Bank data suggest that infant mortality rate (per 1000 child births) has declined from 81 (1990) to 47 (2011).

However, these impressive data on reduction of poverty are not corroborated by other indicators. Normally, reduction of poverty is associated with reduction in unemployment. The rate of unemployment has increased from 7.3% (1991) to 9.8% (2012). The large gap between poverty (about 30%) and unemployment (about 10%) does not tell the full story of economic life. Moreover, there is a high incidence of disguised unemployment: employment in low income activities and in extremely low productivity. The bulk of unemployment is in the rural sector, most of them being landless wage labourers. In 1980, agriculture contributed 38% to GDP; in 2012, it was only 14%, which is on the expected lines. But still, in 2010, 51% were employed in agriculture. India has had a jobless growth during the last two decades: only 1.36% growth in jobs in the urban areas and negative (-0.38%) in rural areas. The conventional expectation regarding the transition from agriculture to industry has not happened during the two decades of economic reform.

Even if we accept that the income of the poor has gone up during the last two decades, it is not reflected in their lifestyle. It has been calculated by an economist that an average poor family has 100 kilograms of less food in 2007 compared to 1997.[2] More farmers are committing suicides due to debt: on an average of 15 per hour. Agrarian distress has increased manifold. While pointing out that in the 1990s the agricultural elites have moved towards a capitalist model of agriculture, Vakulabharanam and Motiram point out that the number of small-holders who constitute a vast majority in the agrarian population "…. has now been dragged into the green revolution model that is slowing down even as the state unevenly tampers with its support structures. They come increasingly into the orbit of informal credit markets that further exacerbate their distress."[3]

The condition of the urban poor does not present a rosy picture either. "[W]hile [the] slum dwellers and young workers express a degree of satisfaction that they are better off as a result of harder work in the present, they point to persistent inequality, insecurity and disparity, and particularly the paucity of present opportunities and the lack of future prospects for themselves."[4] This is in sharp contrast to various avenues of upward mobility for the middle class. In the midst of highly fluid and insecure work, the poor have become 'reluctant entrepreneurs' by informal self-employment, which is due to distress and not because of incentives offered by a new urban economic milieu. They tend to struggle at the lowest rungs of urban economy.

Inequality

It has been widely alleged that the idea of 'inclusive growth' has remained a myth. The gap between India and Bharat, between haves and have-nots, has widened considerably. During the last two decades, the income of the top ten percent of the population has grown at the rate of 3.3% per annum; whereas the same figure for the bottom ten percent is 0.7%. Weisskopf[5] reviewed all the studies on income inequality in India and the following conclusions can be drawn from his analysis. Inequality in rural consumption has been higher in post-reform period since 1991 than in the two previous decades. The same is the case with the urban sector as well; but the latter has a significantly higher degree of inequality compared to the rural population. Per capita consumption by the urban poor in the 1990s increased only half as much as the per capita national average rate of growth of consumer expenditure. Pro-rich bias in the post-reform period was even more striking in the urban than in the rural sector. The urban/rural ratio of average per capita consumption in the post-reform period was significantly higher for the richer than for poorer groups—indicating that in the post-reform period a disproportionate share of the consumption gains went to better-off urban population. Quoting Topalova (2008), Weisskopf summarises, "all measures point to a significant increase in overall inequality in the 1990s, particularly in urban areas, and that … the top of the population enjoyed a substantially larger share of the gains from economic growth compared to the previous decade."[6] During this period, the wealthiest 10% held roughly 50% of total assets, while the bottom 10% held roughly 0.4% of the total assets.

There have been many studies analysing the rising level of regional inequality in post-reform India.[7] There is a broad agreement that inequality among states has increased. "While advanced Industrial states tended to leapfrog in the reform years, other states have lagged behind. ….Unfortunately, backward states with a higher population growth are not able to attract investment—both public and private—due to a variety of reasons, like poor income and infrastructure and probably also poor governance."[8] States in the south and in the west have had a much rapid rate of development than those in the north and in the eastt. Moreover, census figures indicate that population growth in the latter has been higher, thus contributing to further inequality.

There has been a great deal of disparity in economic investments. In the 1990s, out of all the investment proposals received, forward states accounted for about two-thirds of the resources, while the backward states accounted for only about 28%. 36.7% of the proposals of investment were meant only for Maharashtra and Gujarat, which is more than that of all the backward states combined.[9] 75% of the foreign direct investment went to only five states in the 1990s. 63% of the disbursements of the all-India financial institutions as well as 65% of bank credits went to the developed states. The bank credit share of Tamil Nadu exceeds all the credits to poorer states put together.[10] In general, forward states are better administered and have better infrastructure. The state leadership has successfully marketed the states in India and abroad. Therefore, forward states are able to attract the private sector to invest in their states. However, it has been found that when economic variables like per-capita expenditure and poverty ratio are combined with other social variables like literacy rate, education enrolment index, infant mortality rate, life expectancy, access to safe water and access to housing, there is no evidence of rising inter-state inequality in the 1990s.[11]

Possible impacts of economic reform on inequality may go beyond socio-economic differences. There has been a rise in the rural-urban divide. In the 1990s average per capita consumption expenditure in rural areas rose by 8.7%, whereas it rose by 16.6% in urban areas. Part of an explanation of this trend is the movement of workers from farm to non-farm activities and, therefore, migration from rural to urban areas. There is also an increased migration from the backward states to the urban areas of the forward states in search of lucrative assignments. This has been a politically sensitive trend, since parties have lost elections if only urban India was shining. Every government takes extra care to ensure that rural areas are looked after well. This has led to another divide: relatively more public funds go to rural areas than to urban areas.

Economic reform has also resulted in other structural inequalities. There has been a decline of certain occupations and a rise in others.

For instance, sectors like power loom, edible oil, growing of cotton, traditional fishing have declined. But there has been an IT boom. Telecommunication, transport and energy sectors have grown rapidly. Cash crops, floriculture and horticulture have expanded. With the changing occupational patterns, certain types of workers have experienced hidden hardships: seasonal labour migration leading to disruption of family life, spread of HIV-AIDS, irregular school attendance by the children of the migrant laborers, IT workers' work in night shifts and consequent health issues, etc. Also, there is a trend towards informalisation of the labour market and it has an impact on longer working hours, higher insecurity and poorer working conditions. There is also a strong correlation between the highly developed states and gender inequality. There is decline in female-male ratio among the children in the developed states, thanks to the easy affordability of neo-natal tests.

Besides regional inequality, certain areas and groups have been negatively affected by the economic reforms. These are primarily tribal and forest areas. The private sector has been eager to exploit these areas in acquiring raw materials without a corresponding attention for developing these areas. There is a clear trend towards environmental degradation. Uneven development of these areas has led to Maoist violence. The only silver lining in regional inequality is that the rich states could have a demonstration effect on the less developed ones and would strive to be achievers instead of going to New Delhi all the time with a begging bowl.

Implications for Politics

'Poverty' and 'inequality' are as much political vocabularies as economic. Volumes have been written by economists on the strategies for reducing poverty and inequality or whether benefits of economic reform have percolated downwards. We will not join this debate. There seems to be a broad consensus, however, that during the first two decades of economic reform the level of poverty has declined marginally; but inequality has increased. Everyone has benefited somewhat, though the rich and middle class have gained more than others.

What worries a student of political science is that about one-third of the Indian population is below poverty line, most of them unemployed or underemployed. This number is good enough to make or break a government. It is the good luck of the political elite that the 'poor' in India are not a socially homogeneous category. Their identity has got enmeshed in various other segments based on caste, religion, region or ethnicity. How does this affect the politics in a competitive political economy?

First, political discourse has become essentially negative. In a nationalist political economy attempts were made to address the needs of all the poor, irrespective of their primordial identities. In a populist political economy, the 'vote bank' of a party was clearly defined; a voter knew what to expect, or otherwise. Now the politics centres round the extent of 'deprivation'. For example, Adivasis are deprived of access to forests, displaced persons are deprived of their land, urban poor are deprived of clean drinking water, rural children are deprived of access to education, women are deprived of safety in the work place etc. The list could be very long. The crux of the matter is that different segments of population are organising themselves around these deprivations. It is true that there have been legislations to address some of these issues, e.g., NREGA, RTE, RTI, Food Security Bill etc. However, most of the discussions on these measures take note of the 'deprivations' suffered by specific segments. Individuals get these benefits as a right, not as a charity. However, if any segment is left out, feels deprived. These deprivations—not welfare—have become electorally salient issues.

There is a second related issue. These segments clearly understand that the task of politics is to bargain, negotiate and extract benefits as a right. They would not surrender their votes to a vote bank. Therefore, their political identity is not blindly attached to a political party. Political market today is as competitive as an economic market. A segment's numerical strength and perceived deprivations enhance its bargaining potential. It can shift to any party or coalition based on a calculus of political benefits and costs. Ideological commitments are *passé.* Such realignments are taking place not only at the level of local politics, but also in the national level, where state and regional leaders bargain without any hesitation.[12] We will turn to the latter in the next chapter.

Notes

1. Arvind Panagariya, *India: The Emerging Giant* (New York: Oxford University Press, 2008), pp. 130-1.
2. Utsa Patnaik's estimate quoted in P. Sainath, "Largest Wave of Suicides in History", *Counterpunch,* February 12, 2009.
3. V. Vakulabharanam and S. Motiram, "Political Economy of Agrarian Distress in India since the 1990s" in Sanjay Ruparelia et al (eds.), *Understanding India's New Political Economy* (London: Routledge, 2011), p. 123.
4. Nandini Gooptu, "Economic Liberalization, Urban Politics and the Poor" in ibid, p. 45.
5. Thomas E. Weisskopf, "Why Worry about Inequality in the Booming Indian Economy?", *Economic and Political Weekly*, XLVI (47), November 19, 2011.
6. Ibid, p.46.
7. N. J. Kurian, "Widening Regional Disparities in India", *Economic and Political Weekly*, February 12, 2000; Nirvikar Singh, Lavesh Bhandari, Aoyu Chen and Aarti Khare, "Regional Inequality in India: A Fresh Look", *Economic and Political Weekly*, March 15, 2003; S.L. Shetty, "Growth of SDP and Structural Changes In the State Economies" *Economic and Political Weekly*, December 6, 2003; and B.B. Bhattacharya and S. Saktivel, "Regional Growth and Disparity in India: Comparison of Pre- and Post-Reform Decades", *Economic and Political Weekly*, March 6, 2004.
8. Bhattacharya and Saktivel, ibid, p. 1077.
9. Kurian, ibid, p. 545.
10. Amaresh Bagchi and John Kurian, "Regional Inequalities in India: Pre- and Post-Reform Trends and Challenges for Policy" in Jos Mooij (ed.), *Poilitics of Economic Reform in India* (New Delhi: Sage, 2005), p. 338.
11. Panagariya, op.cit., p. 162.
12. Bihar's plank on economic deprivation, Telangana's slogans on developmental deprivations or a tribal group's lack of access to the forest produce use similar political language.

9. Economic Reform and the Emergence of a Competitive Federal Polity

Scholars have always been perplexed by the nature of Indian federalism. While the Indian Constitution has provided a fine blueprint of clear division of powers between Centre and the states, the actual working of relationship between the two structures of power has been far from straightforward. During the first few decades after independence the autonomy and power of the states was often compromised due to domination by a single party both in the Centre and the states. The institutional arrangements ensured the states' economic subordination as well. The Centre had access to more resources, which it disbursed to the states through centralised institutions like the Finance Commission and the Planning Commission. The Centre had the primary responsibility of deciding the locations of big industries, irrigation projects etc. Therefore, India looked like a centralised federation. Since the Centre can hardly ground any of its plans and programmes without the cooperation from the relevant states, India has been also regarded as an example of cooperative federalism.

By the 1990s, however, both the political and economic scenario had changed dramatically. One-party system gave way to a multi-party system, with several regional parties functioning actively.[1] Many state-level leaders became important leaders at the Centre because of the logic of coalition politics. Several aspects of the economic reforms allowed the states to exercise autonomy in deciding on its resource mobilisation from national and international sources and design its own strategy of industrialisation. This led to a redefinition of the relationship between the Centre and the states. Among the interpretations on the recent developments in India, the following are prominent. Rob Jenkins has suggested that federalism has helped to reduce political opposition to reforms since there was no unanimity among the states on various issues.[2] Susanne and Lloyd Rudolph have narrated the arrival of a federal market economy replacing the centralised command economy.[3] Lawrence Saez has argued that economic reforms have led to inter-jurisdictional competition among states replacing inter-governmental cooperation.[4] Aseema Sinha thinks that a vertical competition in India's federal system was always there; now a horizontal competition has been added.[5]

Federalism Facilitating Reform

Rob Jenkins argues that India's federal system facilitated the safe launching of economic reform. Economic reforms had uneven effects on the states. Some tended to derive significantly higher benefits while others did not. "Politicians from states that benefit [from economic reforms] have little motivations to oppose reform. Those from states that suffer relative decline in economic performance (or autonomy in determining economic policy) have both less clout and fewer allies with which to mount a serious challenge to liberalisation."[6] These divisions among the states were exploited by the Centre while introducing reforms. A state's economic fate is no longer linked to other states through a centralised planning process. There is no rationale for all the states to collectively fight against the domination of the Centre. Rather there is a process of 'provincial Darwinism' that reduced the effectiveness of states to fight. Competition among the rich and the poor states created a hiatus in the elites' perception of reform process. The former were excited by their new-found power to invite industries to their states, effectively snatching the control hitherto exercised by the Centre. "[*C*]*entre-state* conflict has been partially displaced by *inter-state* competition for inward investment."[7] (emphasis in the original)

Second, since each state became a battleground on the fight over sustainability of economic reforms, political interests got fragmented on regional lines. Conflicts were 'quarantined' within each of the states. Given India's diversity, group conflicts have been confined to a small geographical area. Responses to the same reforms varied from state to state. Such conflicts, therefore, never affected decision-making at the Centre. Dynamics of implementation of reforms—which happens at the state levels—remained divorced from the policy-making process.

Finally, different levels of government allowed political groups to take ambiguous positions: one stand on the approval of a policy and the other for the information to the electorate. A policy could be supported at the state level, while being opposed at the Centre, or vice versa. Sometimes while accommodating a policy at the state level, a party may present a public image of arm-twisting by the Centre. Further, states imitated the successful implementation of a policy in another state to convince their own electorate to accept it. Since in a federal system every state has some autonomy in implementing policies, it is easy to imitate the model of a successful state rather than suggesting that it is a dictate from the Centre. "This often takes place in a rather diffuse and general manner: state-level governing elites may simply discover from studying their neighbours that, in principle, it is possible to retain a traditional electoral base despite ideological reversals."[8]

Federal Market Economy

The Rudolphs associate the economic reforms in India with the emergence of a federal market economy with decision making powers shared between the Centre and the states. Each state shares economic sovereignty and has autonomy and responsibility to effect economic growth. Pointing out to the new role of the Chief Ministers, Rudolphs write, "Not only do they need to negotiate a path that avoids undue capitulation to populist pressures; to invite private investment, they must work in consonance with the centre's new role as a regulator and fiscal disciplinarian and deal with the hard budget constraints demanded by the faceless, international credit-rating agencies."[9] The Chief Ministers have become new entrepreneurs trying to attract domestic and foreign investments. Along with decentralisation of the market, economic sovereignty is shared between the states and the Centre for economic and financial decision-making.

Each state now plays the role of a viable economic unit. The Centre's contribution to the states' capital formation has declined. By coincidence, during the same time, the regionalisation of politics, allowed the states to have their own economic agenda. These economic aspirations could not always be fulfilled by declining public funding. This has provided space to the private investments to contribute to a state's growth. Each state tries to compete with others to attract private investment by bold policy initiatives, imaginative leadership and good governance. Those states which have been able to attract private investments have experienced a higher growth rate than others. In order to compete in this economic race, successful states have given concessions and incentives to business houses as well as provided good work culture with a skilled labour force; good infrastructure, especially power, transport and communication; and good governance.

The states have become less dependent on the Centre for formulation and execution of their economic policies. The Centre has fewer opportunities to intervene and control public investment in states. But it has acquired a new role to regulate market imperfections and ensure the states' fiscal discipline. "As the centre's role as an interventionist state has faded, its role as regulatory state has grown. The centre has attempted to impose hard budget constraints on the states. So too have market-oriented international and domestic credit rating agencies."[10] The new-found economic sovereignty by the states is further curtailed by the fiscal discipline imposed by international lenders such as the World Bank, Asian Development Banketc.

Nature of Competition among the States

Aseema Sinha suggests that during the pre-reform era there was cooperation among the states and domination by the Centre. There was vertical competition: the states competed with each other for centrally determined resources. The post-reform era is characterised by a horizontal competition: states compete with each other more directly and for resources from a wide variety of actors. Convergence of policy discourses around reform, irrespective of previous ideological differences among parties, generated competition among states. In the race to woo investors, the states tried their best to project a good image by highlighting their impressive growth rates or fine credit ratings. They used the media to advertise their industrial policies and achievements. They openly compared themselves to their competitor states. Aggressive marketing and image building became order of the day. Such competition stretched beyond the borders as well. States started to negotiate with foreign governments, multinational corporations and outside investors. The states "play an increasing role in bargaining with international actors to attract foreign direct investment and pursue global integration. Direct attraction of foreign investment by states has contributed to de facto authority to approve foreign investment projects, establish tax rates for foreign investment firms, and establish rules of the game."[11] The states have become participants in giving shape to foreign economic relations. However, while the states compete with each other for their share of the market, they all "continue to rely on state-led strategies of reform; there is no 'Washington Consensus' or 'neoliberal' route to reform in India."[12] Each state guided and created its own strategy of reform. Each one of them relied on its inherited past strategies as well as the political and economic resources found in the state. The Centre and states have realised their changing role in economic development. Policy diffusion has helped each unit to assess its own pace of reforms as well as transforming incentives to the rulers. "India's economic reforms reordered erstwhile centre-state relations, displacing both power and responsibilities to the regional states. However, institutions of the license-quota raj—local institutional capacities and preexisting behaviour patterns dictate—shaped these strategies in diverse ways: change and continuity coexist in post-transition India."[13]

Lawrence Saez argues that the simultaneous impact of two transformations—political party realignment and economic liberalisation—has altered the traditional structure of federal relations in India. There is an apparent decline in the role of the Central government in determining a state's trajectory of economic development. Saez argues that this change "could encourage greater opportunities for grassroots local development and increased inter-jurisdictional cooperation, the impact of massive foreign investment inflows will instead push the debates about federalism in a different direction. This incrementally altered trajectory is from inter-governmental cooperation towards inter-jurisdictional competition."[14] He defines inter-jurisdictional competition as 'the rivalrious and contentious relationship for resources among similar tiers of government or among localities within a region.' This competition is reflected in each geographical area—even a city—trying to attract foreign direct investment (FDI), investment by NRIs or providing incentives for industrialisation. Economic liberalisation has disproportionately benefited middle-income and high-income states, creating a clear divide between what Saez calls as foreign investment magnets and foreign investment laggards. The states which have had a high degree of openness within their jurisdictions have experienced higher rates of growth. At the same time the FDI laggards have tried to compete and improve their economic performance. The influx of foreign investment inflows has gradually diminished the importance of Central government as a principal source of revenues for some states. The Centre has simultaneously lost its dominant role in cementing cooperation between different units of government. There is a need to create new institutions to manage inter-jurisdictional competition, taking into account the greater importance of powerful states, rather than treating them as equals as per the constitutional arrangements. There is a potential danger, however, that such financial disparities could create new forms of domestic unrest. These shifts in political and socio-economic structure could generate new forms of conflicts based on caste, religion, language or ethnicity.

Implications for Politics

As in the case of micro-level politics, competition has been infused at the macro-level, with each state exercising its new-found autonomy by exploring its bargaining potential vis-à-vis other states and the Centre. The earlier model of hierarchy—where the Centre dictated the terms of political patronage—has lost its relevance. Leaders imitate the nature of competition in an economic market. They tried to protect their bargaining potential and have been guided by their own and the state's interests.[15]

Soon after independence, the challenge before India was to integrate in spite of her multiple diversities. The slogan used to be the giving up of 'narrow' interests and discovering the common thread that could bind this subcontinent and create a national identity. Now politics imitates the market, where the players are invariably guided by their own interests. Each state is guided by its own perceived interests. This is not simply competing with other states to attract investors and industries. Conscious attempts are made to prevent other states from exploiting her natural resources. In this political market the Centre is just another player, not a big brother guiding and protecting the states. Voices of states are given importance even in the exclusive domains of the Centre, e.g., relationship with foreign countries.[16] Moreover, this competition is not confined to the states and the Centre, the institutional arrangements defined in the Constitution. Sub-state identities have emerged, each one making their cases to protect interests. There have been numerous demands for new states based on perceived deprivation. Sometimes protection of a state's identities goes beyond her geographical boundaries.[17] However, whether a state's voice will be heard or ignored would depend on her bargaining power based on physical resources and negotiating skills. Therefore, economic reforms have generated a model of bargaining federalism in India.

Notes

1. The recent opposition by the state leaders to Centre's initiative to push through a Bill on multi-brand foreign direct investment or to establish National Counter Terrorism Centre (NCTC) are cases in point.
2. Rob Jenkins, *Democratic Politics and Economic Reforms in India* (Cambridge: Cambridge University Press, 1999) and "How Federalism Influences India's Domestic Politics of WTO Engagement (and is Itself Affected in the Process)", *Asian Survey*, 43, 2003.
3. Llyod I. Rudolph and Susanne H. Rudolph, "The Iconization of Chandrababu: Sharing Sovereignty in India's Federal Market Economy", *Economic and Political Weekly*, May 5, 2001.
4. Lawrence Saez, *Federalism Without a Center: The Impact of Political and Economic Reform on India's Federal System* (New Delhi: Sage, 2002).

5. Aseema Sinha, "The Changing Political Economy of Federalism in India: A Historical Institutionalist Approach", *India Review*, 3 (1), 2004.
6. Ibid, 1999, p. 128.
7. Ibid, p. 135.
8. Ibid, p. 146.
9. Op. cit., in Mukherji (ed), p. 231.
10. Ibid, p. 245.
11. Sinha, op.cit., p. 49.
12. Ibid, p.51.
13. Ibid, p. 56.
14. Lawrence Saez, *Federalism Without A Centre: The Impact of Political and Economic Reform on India's Federal System* (New Delhi: Sage, 2002), pp. 149-50.
15. A case in point is Mamata Banerjee's hard bargaining with the Centre. Another example is the way Congress leaders from Telangana have successfully defied the Congress High Command.
16. Two recent cases: India voted against Sri Lanka in the United Nations Human Rights Council because of pressure from Tamil Nadu (*The Hindu*, March 22, 2012); Kerala's stand in dealing with Italian marines prevailed despite plenty of diplomatic pressure on India from Italy (*The Hindu*, February 16, 2012).
17. Bihar's Chief Minister tries to protect the well-being of Biharis in Mumbai or Odisha's Chief Minister is concerned when Odia labourers are tortured in Surat or Manipuris are agitated when one of their students is killed in Bangalore.

10. Conclusion: Whither Indian Political Economy?

The essence of collective life centres round interests, conflicts and bargaining; in short, around politics, which do not allow a neat economic model to explain the choice of policies. One needs to delineate the distribution of power and wealth between different groups and individuals over time. The process that creates, sustains and transforms this relationship helps us to analyse the nature of political economy in a country.

This monograph is an attempt to understand this complex process formulation of economic policy in India since her independence. We have tried to argue that there is a symbiotic relationship between India's economy and polity. During the initial years of celebration of nationalism, Nehru's charisma and mass support allowed him to freely choose economic policies that were considered to be in 'national interest'. He tried to create a political consensus, instead of calculating political pay-offs for his own party. Such a grand coalition could not be sustained for long, since those who benefited did not sing paeans for Nehru and those who lost became sworn enemies of the Congress party. In short, the political context of nationalism generated a command economy by an interventionist state, which in turn created ruptures and conflicts among various political interests.

Indira Gandhi realised the importance of calculating her political payoffs and nurtured her 'rainbow' coalition consisting of the poor and the marginalised. Politics became polarised: political groups were either with the Congress or against the Congress, unlike the previous period where—except for a few minor parties—all groups were under the umbrella of the Congress party. This political context led to redistributive economic policies which aimed at providing benefits to the presumed supporters of a ruling party. This model of populism was adopted by almost every party in power, whether at the Centre or the states for almost two decades. Instead of trying to get support from a grand coalition, minimum winning coalitions emerged. Political interests became the primary determinant of economic policies. New political classes, beneficiaries of such economic policies, emerged and asserted their power at different levels. Since benefits accrued to specific groups, new groups with new identities emerged, often breaking down the older identities. Redistributive political economy had this ironical twist: economic policies sustained political groups; but political groups could not sustain themselves. Every small group tried to assert its power and looked for a piece of the pie of redistributive policy. This created a system overload, till economic sustenance came to a breaking point. In short, polarised politics led to a redistributive economy, which in turn fragmented politics.

By the time India entered into the last decade of the twentieth century, political uncertainty was rampant. Political groups were so segmented that no political party was in a position to calculate its political payoffs from a certain policy. Most of them were not even sure of the probability of their access to political power and were, therefore hesitant to offer goodies to their own supporters. Each group tried to get a competitive advantage over the others without being sure of its own strength. Each party's preferred position on economic policy was, therefore, fuzzy and flexible. This uncertainty was instrumental in allowing a smooth passage of economic reform proposals from 1991 onwards. A fragmented political context would not obviously allow the state's overarching control over the economy. Each political party was uncertain about the probability of controlling the state's power. It could not possibly allow others to get into that enviable position either. Therefore, the shrinking of the state in favour of the market seemed to be a viable option. A fragmented polity led to liberalisation of the economy and both contributed to the emergence of a new phase of competitive political economy.

To summarise, the grand coalition in the phase of Nationalist Political Economy calculated payoffs for the entire country; the minimum-winning coalition in the phase of Populist Political Economy calculated payoffs of the supporters of the ruling party; and the uncertainty on the possibility of any coalition formation in the phase of Competitive Political Economy made it difficult to calculate political payoffs. Economic reforms were the result of this political uncertainty.

Whither India's Political Economy?

Every phase of political economy has its winners and losers, in terms of power and wealth. But what is common among all the three phases is that decision-making on economic policy has been determined by a political calculus of the ruling class, both in the government and in the opposition. When that calculus changed, economic policy witnessed a radical shift.

It is often alleged that the Indian state has retreated and got weakened in the post-reform phase. In other words, the state is not able to do enough for its citizens, especially those who are marginalised, since the economic resources are controlled by the market forces. The data on Government of India's expenditures on social sector during the post-reform phase, however, indicate a remarkable continuity.[1] Increasing importance of the market forces has not weakened the state. The Indian state may no longer have 'commanding heights' over the economy; but public sector enterprises do exist today. Some of them continue to be giants in the industrial sector. Technically, India is still a mixed economy. The Government of India might have eased a part of its control over industry, trade and commerce. But regulation continues in different guises, e.g., the necessity of obtaining environmental clearances from the Government of India to establish industries. If anything, greater volume of control has shifted to the states, who take care of land acquisition, law and order, labour laws, factory safety laws, provision of infrastructure, etc. Industrialists these days spend more time negotiating at state capitals rather than at the national capital. States are willing and able to take decisions as their institutional assertion of power in the wake of the emergence of a federal market economy. This is just natural since there has been a process of regionalisation of politics and parties.[2] Even politics in New Delhi is controlled by important state leaders, whose local economic agenda influence the national economic policy.

One may suggest that the Indian state has not been weakened; but it has been transformed from a regulatory state to a 'competition' state.[3] First, the post-reform legislations aimed at promoting competition among the industries and business houses. Several independent regulatory authorities have been established in sectors like telecommunication, electricity etc. A competition commission has been established "to prevent practices having adverse effect on competition, to promote and sustain competition in markets, to protect the interests of consumers and to ensure freedom of trade carried on by other participants in markets"[4]. Even public sector units are facing competition from an open market. Second, the Centre is encouraging competition among the states to promote greater economic activity. Each state is busy marketing itself to woo investors. Earlier corporate houses were queuing up in the corridors of power. Now the state bureaucracy is going to the corporate houses and offering sops like infrastructure, land, favourable tax regime etc. The competition has moved beyond the borders as well. Many Chief Ministers are smart enough to hold open houses abroad to attract foreign investors, especially the NRIs belonging to the same linguistic or ethnic groups. Third, an aspect of India's economic reform is to open up her economy. India now accepts compulsions of the international market and changing technology. This is reversal of the earlier policy of 'export pessimism'. Indian state facilitates the Indian businesses to compete and get their share in the world market. Many Indian corporates are now successful in their international ventures and multinational corporations are comfortably doing business in India. In general, this new economic culture promotes enterprise, innovation and profitability.

The Indian state in the post-independence period symbolised a sense of national solidarity and provided deeper legitimacy to institutionalised power and social embeddedness. It acquired the social and political capacity to pursue economic goals of development. Some of these capacities may have been challenged by India's transformation into a competitive political economy. First, Entrepreneurial Governments have emerged at different levels, from national to local. Political power is not simply confined to the legal power to govern; political entrepreneurs need to market their products before other political actors and the people.

The earlier notion of public ownership as an instrument of political modernisation is being gradually replaced by development initiatives coming from the grassroots. While economy is getting globalised, politics is getting localised. This relationship between the government and the people is based on trust, freedom and responsibility. This transforms the sources of legitimacy of a political authority. A government is seen as a managing partner in delivering policy products. The individuals and groups—the shareholders in this political enterprise—may throw out the managers of a political enterprise, if they cannot deliver. Emotions, passions or ideology do not easily get translated into public policy.

Secondly, a competitive political economy divides and fragments any centralised economic policy. The political actors no longer have a single playing field to maximise the 'public interest', for the scope of public interest itself is in doubt and a survival of any set of winners in politics is uncertain. Political and institutional entrepreneurs, therefore, try their best not merely to adapt, but to control at least parts of the game itself. They seem to be in a hurry to convert their gains to the advantage of their coalition building and constituency attracting activities. It should not surprise us that the rent-seeking political class has expanded during the last couple of decades.

Thirdly, there has been a trend towards the post-welfare state, integrating people into the private sector even in the traditional welfare services like education and healthcare. The state has not abandoned its obligation to provide social security to its citizens; but there has been a general approach to reduce the welfare dependency on the state. For example, there have been attempts to deal with unemployment through the market place, not necessarily through government intervention; the experiment of the policy on rural employment guarantee being an exception. The imperative of competition among political actors has provided a higher ideological status to consumerist values rather than productionist values associated with a centralised planning. The consumer/citizen is the king both in the economic and the political market. This may eventually lead to welfare with a human face rather than services being imposed from above.

The competitive political economy seems to be a mixed bag. The Indian state's role in formulating economic policy is shared with international agencies on one side and different state and local governments on the other. Often policy initiatives come from private sector, international policy networks and NGOs. It gives the appearance of a weak governing structure. However, it is the same apparently weak structure that is able to take hard decisions to share power with others. Political actors, like entrepreneurs in the economic market, are not simply interested to manufacture products, but also to sell them to their clients, the individuals, groups and even to other political actors. While political actors face uncertainty in a competitive political economy, the citizens, as consumers of public policies, are further empowered to question, accept or reject any initiative. This is evident from several grassroot movements in the country during the last decade. Citizens and groups are able to assert their rights and, if necessary, throw out the political entrepreneurs out of business.[5] Rights dominate over welfare in the new policy regime.

Notes

1. Expenditure on Social Sector, including Rural Development was 6.78% of the GDP in 1991-92 budget of GoI; the same was 7.55% in the 1999-2000 budget. The same figures for Social Sector expenditure as % of aggregate total expenditures were 24.85% and 27.69%. These data imply that the allocations were increased slightly during this period. Please see Table 2 of Jos Mooij and S. Mahendra Dev, "Social Sector Priorities: An Analysis of Budgets and Expenditures in India in the 1990s", *Development Policy Review,* 22(1), 2004, pp. 97-120. They also point out that the budget speeches of all finance ministers point out that poverty alleviation is their primary goal. The corresponding figures in 2012-13 budget are 7.09% and 25.01%. [http://indiabudget.nic.in/es2012-13/echap-13.pdf]
2. Prakash Sarangi, "Economic Reform and Party System" in Jos Mooij (ed) *Politics of Economic Reform in India* (New Delhi: Sage, 2005).
3. Phillip G. Cerny, "The Competition State Today", *Policy Studies*, 31 (1), 2010, pp. 5-21. Cerny writes that the process of emergence of the completion state "does not lead to simple decline of the state but may be seen to necessitate the actual expansion of *de facto* state intervention and regulation in the name of competitiveness and marketisation.", "Paradoxes of the Competition State: the Dynamics of Political Globalization", *Government and Opposition*, 32 (2), 1997, p. 215.
4. http://www.cci.gov.in/index.php?option=com_content&task=view&id=120

5. In the recent past, there have been many instances of incumbents in state governments losing power in elections. The so called 'anti-incumbency' factor is a euphemism for poor governance. Now there are many cases of parties with good record of governance getting reelected. Machiavelli said long back that an innovator cannot win simply with guns and forts; the innovations (new policies) need to be liked by people. "… nothing is harder to manage, more risky in undertaking, or more doubtful of success than to set up as the introducer of a new order", Nicolo Machiavelli, *The Prince*, Ch. VI.

Bibliography

Ahluwalia, Montek S., "India's Economic Reforms" in Robert Cassen and Vijay Joshi (eds.), *India: The Future of Economic Reform* (Delhi: Oxford University Press, 1995).

Ahluwalia, Montek S., "Economic Reforms in India since 1991: Has Gradualism Worked?" in Rahul Mukherji (ed), *India's Economic Transition: The Politics of Reforms* (Oxford: Oxford University Press, 2007).

Bagchi, Amaresh and John Kurian, "Regional Inequalities in India: Pre- and Post-Reform Trends and Challenges for Policy" in Jos Mooij (ed), *Poilitics of Economic Reform in India* (New Delhi: Sage, 2005).

Bagchi, Amiya Kumar, "From a Fractured Compromise to a Democratic Consensus: Planning and Political Economy in Post-Colonial India", *Economic and Political Weekly,* Vol. 26, No. 11/12, pp. 611-628, March 1991.

Bardhan, Pranab, *Political Economy of Development in India*, 2nd edition, (New Delhi: Oxford University Press, 1999).

Bardhan, Pranab, "Notes on the Political Economy of India's Tortuous Transition", *Economic and Political Weekly,* Vol. 44, No. 49, pp. 31-36, December 5, 2009.

Basu, Kaushik, "India's Dilemmas: The Political Economy of Policy Making in a Globalized World", *Economic and Political Weekly,* Vol. 43, No. 5, pp. 53-62, February 2, 2008.

Bhagwati, Jagdish, *India in Transition: Freeing the Economy* (Oxford: Clarendon Press, 1993).

Bhagwati, Jagdish, "What Went Wrong?" in Rahul Mukherji (ed), *India's Economic Transition* (New Delhi: OUP, 2007).

Bhagwati, Jagdish and Arvind Panagariya, *India's Tryst with Destiny:*

Debunking Myths that Undermine Progress and Addressing New Challenges (New Delhi: HarperCollins, 2012).

Bhagwati, Jagdish and Arvind Panagariya (eds.), *India's Reforms: How they Produced Inclusive Growth* (New York: Oxford University Press, 2012).

Bhattacharya, B.B. and S. Saktivel, "Regional Growth and Disparity in India: Comparison of Pre- and Post-Reform Decades", *Economic and Political Weekly*, March 6, 2004.

Buchanan, James M. and Gordon Tullock, *The Calculus of Consent* (Ann Arbor: The University of Michigan Press, 1962).

Caporaso, James A. and David P. Levine, *Theories of Political Economy* (Cambridge: Cambridge University Press, 1992).

Carras, Mary C., *Indira Gandhi: In the Crucible of Leadership: A Political Biography* (Boston: Beacon Press, 1979).

Cerny, Phillip G., "Paradoxes of the Competition State: the Dynamics of Political Globalization", *Government and Opposition*, 32 (2), 1997.

Cerny, Phillip G., "The Competition State Today", *Policy Studies*, 31 (1), 2010.

Chakravarty, Sukhamoy, *Development Planning: The Indian Experience* (Oxford: Clarendon Press, 1987).

Downs, Anthony, *An Economic Theory of Democracy* (New York: Harper & Row, 1957).

Frankel, Francine R., *India's Political Economy 1947-2004* (New Delhi: OUP, 2005).

Frey, Bruno S., *Democratic Economic Policy* (New York: St. Martin's Press, 1983).

Gooptu, Nandini, "Economic Liberalization, Urban Politics and the Poor" in Sanjay Ruparelia et al (eds.), *Understanding India's New Political Economy* (London: Routledge, 2011).

Hall, Peter A. and Rosemary C.R. Taylor, "Political Science and the Three New Institutionalisms", *Political Studies*, XLIV, 1996.

Hardgrave, Robert L., Jr. and Stanley A. Kochanek, *India: Government and Politics in a Developing Nation* (Boston: Thomson Wadsworth, 2008).

Jenkins, Rob, *Democratic Politics and Economic Reform in India* (Cambridge: Cambridge University Press, 1999).

Jenkins, Rob, "How Federalism Influences India's Domestic Politics of WTO Engagement (and is Itself Affected in the Process)", *Asian Survey*, 43, 2003.

Joshi, P.C., *Land Reforms in India* (New Delhi: Institute of Economic Growth, 1975).

Joshi, Vijay and I.M.D. Little, *India's Economic Reforms 1991-2001* (Oxford: Clarendon Press, 1996).

Kochanek, Stanley A., *The Congress Party of India* (Princeton: Princeton University Press, 1968).

Kochanek, Stanley A, "Liberalization and Business Lobbying in India", *Journal of Commonwealth and Comparative Politics*, 34(3), 1996.

Kohli, Atul, *The State and Poverty in India* (Cambridge: Cambridge University Press, 1987).

Kohli, Atul, *Democracy and Development in India* (New Delhi: Oxford University Press, 2009).

Kurian, N. J., "Widening Regional Disparities in India", *Economic and Political Weekly*, February 12, 2000.

Ladejinsky, Wolf, *Agrarian Reform as Unfinished Business* (London: Oxford University Press, 1977).

Lindblom, Charles E., *Politics and Markets* (New York: Basic Books, 1977).

Lindblom, Charles E., *Democracy and Market System* (Oslo: Norwegian University Press, 1988).

Nayar, Baldev Raj, *India's Mixed Economy* (Bombay: Popular Prakashan, 1989).

Nayar, Baldev Raj, *Globalization and Nationalism: The Changing Balance in India's Economic Policy, 1950-2000* (New Delhi: Sage, 2001).

Nayyar, Deepak, "Economic Development and Political Democracy: Interaction of Economics and Politics in Independent India", *Economic and Political Weekly of India*, December 5, 1998.

North, Douglass C., *Institutions, Institutional Change and Economic*

Performance (New York: Cambridge University Press, 1990).

Panagariya, Arvind, *India: The Emerging Giant* (New York: Oxford University Press, 2008).

Persson, Torsten and Guido Tabellini, *Political Economics*, (Cambridge: The MIT Press, 2000).

Przeworski, Adam, *States and Markets: A Primer in Political Economy* (Cambridge: Cambridge University Press, 2003).

Rudolph, Lloyd I. and Susanne H. Rudolph, *In Pursuit of Lakshmi: The Political Economy of the Indian State* (Chicago: University of Chicago Press, 1987).

Rudolph, Llyod I. and Susanne H. Rudolph, "The Iconization of Chandrababu: Sharing Sovereignty in India's Federal Market Economy", *Economic and Political Weekly*, May 5, 2001.

Sachs, Jeffrey D., Ashutosh Varshney and Nirupam Bajpai (eds.), *India in the Era of Economic Reform* (New Delhi: Oxford University Press, 1999).

Saez, Lawrence, *Federalism Without a Center: The Impact of Political and Economic Reform on India's Federal System* (New Delhi: Sage, 2002).

Sainath, P., "Largest Wave of Suicides in History", *Counterpunch*, February 12, 2009.

Sarangi, Prakash, "Economic Reform and Party System" in Jos Mooij (ed) *Politics of Economic Reform in India* (New Delhi: Sage, 2005).

Sharma, Shalendra D., *Development and Democracy in India* (Boulder: Lynne Rienner, 1999).

Shetty, S.L., "Growth of SDP and Structural Changes In the State Economies", *Economic and Political Weekly*, December 6, 2003.

Singh, Manmohan, "India's Economic Reforms: The Experience and Options" in R.K. Sinha (ed), *India's Economic Reforms and Beyond* (New Delhi: Anamika Publishers, 1995).

Singh, Nirvikar, Lavesh Bhandari, Aoyu Chen and Aarti Khare, "Regional Inequality in India: A Fresh Look", *Economic and Political Weekly*, March 15, 2003.

Sinha, Aseema, "The Changing Political Economy of Federalism in

India: A Historical Institutionalist Approach", *India Review*, 3 (1), 2004.

Subramaniam, K.N., "A Balance Sheet", *Seminar*, 304, December 1984.

Tendulkar, Suresh D. and T.A. Bhavani, *Understanding Reforms: Post-1991 India* (New Delhi: Oxford University Press, 2007).

Vakulabharanam V. and S. Motiram, "Political Economy of Agrarian Distress in India since the 1990s" in Sanjay Ruparelia et al (eds.), *Understanding India's New Political Economy* (London: Routledge, 2011).

Varshney, Ashutosh, "Mass Politics or Elite Politics? India's Economic Reforms in Comparative Perspective" in Jeffrey D. Sachs et al (eds.), *India in the Era of Economic Reforms* (New Delhi: Oxford University Press, 1999).

Warriner, Doreen, *Land Reform in Principle and Practice* (Oxford Clarendon Press, 1969).

Weingast, Barry R. and Donald A. Wittman, *The Oxford Handbook of Political Economy* (Oxford: Oxford University Press, 2006).

Weisskopf, Thomas E., "Why Worry about Inequality in the Booming Indian Economy?", *Economic and Political Weekly*, XLVI (47), November 19, 2011.

Index